WAR AND PEACE

Borgo Press Books Edited & Translated by FRANK J. MORLOCK

Alcestis: A Play in Five Acts, by Philippe Quinault * *Anna Karenina: A Play in Five Acts*, by Edmond Guiraud, from Leo Tolstoy * *Anthony: A Play in Five Acts*, by Alexandre Dumas, Père * *Atys: A Play in Five Acts*, by Philippe Quinault * *The Boss Lady: A Play in Five Acts*, by Paul Féval, Père * *The Children of Captain Grant: A Play in Five Acts*, by Jules Verne & Adolphe d'Ennery * *Cleopatra: A Play in Five Acts*, by Victorien Sardou * *Crime and Punishment: A Play in Three Acts*, by Frank J. Morlock, from Fyodor Dostoyevsky * *Don Quixote: A Play in Three Acts*, by Victorien Sardou, from Miguel de Cervantes * *The Dream of a Summer Night: A Fantasy Play in Three Acts*, by Paul Meurice * *Falstaff: A Play in Four Acts*, by William Shakespeare, John Dennis, William Kendrick, & Frank J. Morlock * *The Idiot: A Play in Three Acts*, by Frank J. Morlock, from Fyodor Dostoyevsky * *Isis: A Play in Five Acts*, by Philippe Quinault * *Jesus of Nazareth: A Play in Three Acts*, by Paul Demasy * *The Jew of Venice: A Play in Five Acts*, by Ferdinand Dugué * *Joan of Arc: A Play in Five Acts*, by Charles Desnoyer * *The Lily of the Valley: A Play in Five Acts*, by Théodore Barrière & Arthur de Beauplan, from Honoré de Balzac * *Lord Byron in Venice: A Play in Three Acts*, by Jacques Ancelot * *Louis XIV and the Affair of the Poisons: A Play in Five Acts*, by Victorien Sardou * *The Man Who Saw the Devil: A Play in Two Acts*, by Gaston Leroux * *Mathias Sandorf: A Play in Three Acts*, by Jules Verne & William Busnach * *Michael Strogoff: A Play in Five Acts*, by Jules Verne & Adolphe d'Ennery * *Les Misérables: A Play in Two Acts*, by Victor Hugo, Paul Meurice, & Charles Victor Hugo * *Monte Cristo, Part One: A Play in Five Acts*, by Alexandre Dumas, Père * *Monte Cristo, Part Two: A Play in Five Acts*, by Alexandre Dumas, Père * *Monte Cristo, Part Three: A Play in Five Acts*, by Alexandre Dumas, Père * *Monte Cristo, Part Four: A Play in Five Acts*, by Alexandre Dumas, Père * *The Musketeers: A Play in Five Acts*, by Alexandre Dumas, Père * *The Mysteries of Paris: A Play in Five Acts*, by Eugène Sue & Prosper Dinaux * *Napoléon Bonaparte: A Play in Six Acts*, by Alexandre Dumas, Père * *Ninety-Three: A Play in Four Acts*, by Victor Hugo & Paul Meurice * *Notes from the Underground: A Play in Two Acts*, by Frank J. Morlock, from Fyodor Dostoyevsky * *Outrageous Women: Lady MacBeth and Other French Plays*, edited by Frank J. Morlock * *Peau de Chagrin: A Play in Five Acts*, by Louis Judicis, from Honoré de Balzac * *The Prisoner of the Bastille: A Play in Five Acts*, by Alexandre Dumas, Père * *A Raw Youth: A Play in Five Acts*, by Frank J. Morlock, from Fyodor Dostoyevsky * *Richard Darlington: A Play in Three Acts*, by Alexandre Dumas, Père * *The San Felice: A Play in Five Acts*, by Maurice Drack, from Alexandre Dumas, Père * *Saul and David: A Play in Five Acts*, by Voltaire * *Shylock, the Merchant of Venice: A Play in Three Acts*, by Alfred de Vigny * *Socrates: A Play in Three Acts*, by Voltaire * *The Son of Porthos: A Play in Five Acts*, by Émile Blavet, from M. Paul Mahalin * *The Stendhal Hamlet Scenarios and Other Shakespearean Shorts from the French*, edited by Frank J. Morlock * *A Summer Night's Dream: A Play in Three Acts*, by Joseph-Bernard Rosier & Adolphe de Leuwen * *The Three Musketeers: A Play in Five Acts*, by Alexandre Dumas, Père * *Urbain Grandier and the Devils of Loudon: A Play in Four Acts*, by Alexandre Dumas, Père * *The Voyage Through the Impossible: A Play in Three Acts*, by Jules Verne & Adolphe d'Ennery * *War and Peace: A Play in Five Acts*, by J. W. Bienstock & Charles Martel * *The Whites and the Blues: A Play in Five Acts*, by Alexandre Dumas, Père * *William Shakespeare: A Play in Six Acts*, by Ferdinand Dugué

WAR AND PEACE
A Play in Five Acts

by

J. Wladimir Bienstock and Charles Martel
Translated and Adapted by Frank J. Morlock

The Borgo Press

An Imprint of Wildside Press LLC

MMX

Copyright © 2009, 2010 by Frank J. Morlock

All rights reserved. No part of this book may be reproduced without the expressed written consent of the author. Professionals are warned that this material, being fully protected under the copyright laws of the United States of America, and all other countries of the Berne and Universal Copyright Convention, is subject to a royalty. All rights, including all forms of performance now existing or later invented, but not limited to professional, amateur, recording, motion picture, recitation, public reading, radio, television broadcasting, DVD, and Role Playing Games, and all rights of translation into foreign languages, are expressly reserved. Particular emphasis is placed on the question of readings, and all uses of these plays by educational institutions, permission for which must be secured in advance from the author's publisher, Wildside Press, 9710 Traville Gateway Dr. #234, Rockville, MD 20850 (phone 301-762-1305).

www.wildsidebooks.com

FIRST WILDSIDE EDITION

CONTENTS

Cast of Characters 7

Act I, Scene 1 11
Act II, Scene 2 37
Act II, Scene 3: Vilna 63
Act III, Scene 4 71
Act III, Scene 5: After Smolensk 96
Act IV, Scene 6 125
Act IV, Scene 7: Borodino 137
Act V, Scene 8 141
Act V, Scene 9 152
Act V, Scene 10 161

About the Editor 165

DEDICATION

TO THE MEMORY OF LEO TOLSTOI (1828-1910),
WHOSE EPIC NOVEL ON WHICH THIS PLAY IS
BASED INFLUENCED ME THROUGHOUT MY LIFE,

AND TO JEAN WLADIMIR BIENSTOCK,
FOR SUCCESSFULLY DRAMATIZING THE NOVEL
WITH GREAT FIDELITY TO THE ORIGINAL

CAST OF CHARACTERS

Count Pierre (or Piotr) Bezhoukov
Prince André Bolkonski
Count Rostov
Petia & Nicholas, his sons
Berg
Prince Basile Kouraguine
Hippolyte & Anatole, his sons
Prince Boris Droubetzkoi
Bilibine
Count Rostopchine
Vicomte de Mortemart
General Dokhtourov
Colonel Nesvitzki
Doctor Metvier
Doctor Lorrain
Aide de Camp to Count Rostopchine
Major Domo
A Priest
A Man in Black
Captain Dolokhov
An Old General
General Balaschov
A Servant of the Rostovs
An Old Soldier
Lieutenant Touchine
Captain Dennisov
Lieutenant Telianine
A sub-officer
A Marshall of Lodgings
General Koutouzov
An Officer
General Volsogen
An Aide de Camp of Koutouzov
Napoleon
Murat
Davoust

An Aide de Camp of Napoleon
A Secretary
1st Chamberlain
2nd Chamberlain
Komarov
Petrov
Fedotov
Makeev
Kysilev
Zikine
Lavrouchka
Tikhone
Bikov
Likhatchov
A Commandant
1st General
2nd General
Vincent Bosse
1st Brancardier
2nd Brancardier
An Officer
1st Passerby
2nd Passerby
3rd Passerby
4th Passerby
A Man
A Madman
1st Functionary
2nd Functionary
Verestchaguine
An Officer
An Ordnance Officer
A Soldier
An Officer
Count Beausset
1st French General
2nd French General
Helene, daughter of Prince Basile
Countess Anna Pavlovna Scherer
Princess Anna Mikhailovna Droubetzkaia
Princess Catherine (Catiche)
Countess Rostov
Natasha, Vera, & Sonia, her daughters
Maria Dmitrievna Afrossimova
Julie Karaguine
Douniacha
A Lady

A Female Merchant
The Major's Wife
Mlle Berthe
A Chambermaid
1st Woman of the People
2nd Woman of the People
Diacre, Children of the choirs
Officers, Servants, Ladies, Marshalls, Generals, Men and Women of the People.

ACT I

Scene 1

A huge salon in the palace of Count Bezhoukov. A large double door opens on the Count's sickroom. A large curtain hides from the audience the interior of this room. Door on the right leading to antechambers. Door on the left leading to interior apartments. On the wall at the right a large portrait of Catherine the Great. In a corner near the entrance an icon before which burns a candle. Sumptuous furniture in the style of Louis XV.

At the back a group of officers. Servants in grand livery.

AT RISE, Countess Scherer is seated on a small divan at the left. Mortemart is standing behind the divan. General Dokhtourov and Colonel Nesvitzki are seated grouped around the Countess. A Lady and a priest are seated on the right—near the portrait of the Empress. Servants come and go. There's a sensation that a great event is taking place in this house.

Priest
The end of terrestrial life has come.

Lady
Think that he's going to die! Count Cyril Vladimirovitch Bezhoukov, such a powerful lord and so rich.

Priest
Death, Madame, knows neither riches nor power. You are doubtless related to the Count?

Lady
No, my father, I don't have that honor. It's my husband who's sending me. We would like to obtain an extension of our rent. The intendant refused it to us, and I've come to request it of the Count himself. But I've come indeed too late. By the way, tell me father—is it time to administer extreme unction?

Priest
The doctors are going to tell us. It's a great sacrament, Madame.

Lady
I know a gentleman who received extreme unction seven times.

Man in Black
(To Major Domo) Well, can I begin to make my preparations?

Major Domo
Would you get out of here. He's not yet dead. I told you I'd inform you.

(The Man in Black vanishes.)

Lady
(To Major Domo) Who are these officers?

Major Domo
It's the military house of the Governor General of Moscow.

Lady
Count Rostopchine is here?

Major Domo
Yes, Madame he just went into His Excellency's room.

(The large double door at the back opens. One of the double doors is held by a valet. Catherine enters in conversation with doctors Lorrain and Metvier. General reaction)

Princess Catherine
(With tears in her eyes) Then he can drink?

Doctor Lorrain
(Looking at his pocket watch) How long has it been since he's taken his medicine?

Princess Catherine
More than an hour, doctor.

Doctor Lorrain
Well in that case take a glass of boiled water and put a pinch of (Gesturing) cremo tartari in it, right colleague?

Doctor Metvier
Exactly!

Princess Catherine
Agreed, doctor! And now, Gentlemen, tell me the truth, I have the strength to hear it.

Doctor Metvier
Alas! Princess there's no example of anyone after the third attack….

Doctor Lorrain
But, still, with the Count's admirable constitution.

Princess Catherine
My uncle has himself asked for Extreme Unction.

Doctor Metvier
Oh, in that case, it's necessary to satisfy his desire.

Princess Catherine
That's fine, gentlemen, I thank you. I am going to give some orders.

Doctor Lorrain
Courage, Princess. We are going to draw up the bulletin for His Majesty and soon we will be with you.

Doctor Metvier
Till soon, Princess. (They bow deeply and head to the right. The Princess goes to the priest and speaks to him in a low voice. He leaves to execute her orders. The lady follows him.)

Doctor Metvier
Don't you think all the same that he might indeed drag it out till tomorrow morning?

Doctor Lorrain
(With a concerted smile) Tonight, not later.

(They leave.)

(Princess Catherine returns and is met by Countess Scherer who takes her hands)

Countess Scherer
My poor Catiche, what frightful moments!

Princess Catherine
Ah, you are nice, Countess. You stayed. I'm going to tell my cousin Basile; he will be very touched.

Countess Scherer
Both of you are admirably devoted. No, I cannot leave at this moment. I'm even going to prolong my stay in Moscow. Her Imperial Majesty wouldn't want it. She has so much affection for your dear uncle.

Princess Catherine
Their Majesties deign to take news twice a day by special courier.

Countess Scherer
Their Majesties have so much kindness! But now, my dear Catiche, that, I've embraced you, I don't want to deprive the sick person of your tenderness. Go prepare the doctor's potion.

(Catiche leaves.)

Countess Scherer
Come on! Now yet another one who's departing. Ah, the eagles of Catherine the Great are no longer numerous. This Bezhoukov, a great figure.

Colonel Nesvitzki
A superb man!

General Dokhtourov
A lion on the battle field.

Countess Scherer
And the most charming conversationalist in the salon. Alas! Monsieur Pierre doesn't resemble him at all.

Mortemart
Who's this Monsieur Pierre.?

Countess Scherer
He's—The Count's son.

Mortemart
I thought Count Bezhoukov was a bachelor.

Countess Scherer
Yes, my dear Mortemart, but you know, these men of the times of Catherine the Great—

General Dokhtourov
There must have been many others—but we only know this one.

Colonel Nesvitzki
In that case, he's the heir?

Countess Scherer
Perhaps but there must surely have been other lovers. Think of it. The finest fortune in Russia—twenty million roubles and more than 40,000 serfs.

Bilibine
(He enters, questions The Major Domo then seeing the Countess rushes to her—and kisses her hand.) Above all Countess, your precious health?

Countess Scherer
Oh, like always. But there's someone here more ill than I am, dear Bilibine.

Bilibine
I know. It's actually on the part of my minister I've come to get news. But the Count doesn't interest me. I am fixed on his fate.

Countess Scherer
You are cynical, Bilibine.

Bilibine
No, dear Countess, I am sincere. In diplomacy, we lie so much in speech and writing, that it's a relief to speak the truth from time to time. Ah, but you know the extraordinary thing? Monsieur Pierre came to Moscow this morning?

Countess Scherer
Why there's nothing extraordinary in that—He came to be present at the last moments of his father.

Bilibine
Hum! He got a bit of a push from the police.

Mortemart
By the police?

Bilibine
He's been expelled from Petersburg.

General Dokhtourov
Come on.

Bilibine
It's the scandal of the season. (All close in, amused.)

Countess Scherer
What did he do, actually?

Bilibine
He chose his friends badly, Him, Prince Anatole—

Countess Scherer
(Pointing to the door.) The son of Prince Basile?

Bilibine
Yes, a certain Dolokhov from the Pavlograd regiment, The Englishman Stievens, and some scamps from the capital, had the idea, after a mad orgy, at the fifteenth bottle of wine from Champagne, of going to find a bear from the circus, and of putting it with them in a carriage, and of getting themselves taken to the home of some actresses—Songs of drunks, screams of women, groans of bears. The police got there to calm them. Then they seized the inspector they tied him back to back with the bear and went to throw them all in the Neva. The bear swims and the inspector kicks—shouting desperately: Stop! Stop! (Laughter)

Mortemart
It's a Russian way of roughing up the watch.

Countess Scherer
I must tell you, Vicomte, that Monsieur Pierre was educated entirely in France.

Countess Scherer
But Alas!—He didn't take up good manners and came back to us impregnated with all the perverse ideas of the Revolution.

General Dokhtourov
(disdainfully) Liberty, Equality, Fraternity!

Nesvitzki
Fevered brain.

Countess Scherer
I am never at ease with him—he says things—

Bilibine
Ah—hell!— He'd really like to play his little Marat—

(André enters; he shakes the hand of two officers. Berg enters followed by a crowd of officers.)

Countess Scherer
Ah—Now there's a defender for Monsieur Pierre.

Colonel Nesvitzki
And a defender of note.

General Dokhtourov
(Leaving the group.) Hello, Bolkonski.

André
(Shaking the general's hand—bowing to the others.) I was looking for Prince Basile.

Countess Scherer
(Who André hadn't noticed at first.) He's with the patient.

André
Ah, Countess, my respects. Have you seen Count Bezhoukov?

Countess Scherer
Yes, I've seen him, alas. It's mourning clothes for your father, his childhood comrade and his companion in arms.

André
Yes, my father is deeply affected. And myself—on account of Pierre.

Countess Scherer
And—Monsieur Pierre. You arrive apropos, my dear Prince—we were in the process of mistreating your friend.

André
Oh, that's not nice, he is so good.

Bilibine
Hum! There's a certain inspector of Police who doesn't find him quite so good.

André
Yes, I know. But that's the fate of his character. He let's himself be led away too easily.

General Dokhtourov
You've known him for a long while?

André
Since childhood. He has his faults—he gets violently carried away like all timid people—distracted to the point of being comical, but honest—righteous even—a heart of gold.

Mortemart
What warmth! He does well to be friends with you.

André
I love Pierre a lot.

Bilibine
(Noticing Berg, he tries to attract his attentions with smile) Heavens, friend Berg—(Aside) He's insinuated himself here, the little German.

Berg
Excellency, you are very nice.

Colonel Nesvitzki
My congratulation. I learned that you were attached to a Major Command.

André
Yes, General Koutouzov indeed wanted me as an Aide de Camp.

Berg
(To Bilibine) Dare I ask you, Excellency, to present me to Prince Bolkonski.

Bilibine
Already? Gladly—my dear Prince, Lieutenant Berg of the Preobrajensky Regiment. He comes from our German provinces; he will go far—

André
Enchanted.

Berg
Dare I ask you Prince, since you are so near the person of General Koutouzov…?

(The large doors open—Rostopchine enters with Catherine and Prince Basile who kisses Catherine's hand and she goes back into the Count's room. Rostopchine comes forward head high without looking at anyone.)

A beautiful page of history is coming to an end, gentlemen.

(To Basile) It's really hard for me to find the hero in this condition. He certainly had something to tell me, I saw it in his look—Didn't you notice that at a certain moment he attempted to make a gesture? But his hand no longer obeyed him. Perhaps you'll be luckier than I and can guess his final wish.

(Shaking Basile's hand.) In the evening I will see my Aide de Camp about it.

(To one of his officers.) You, Captain, be prepared for the legal formalities.

(He leaves with his staff and servants. Prince Basile goes toward Countess Scherer's group and shakes hands.)

(Prince Basile approaches the Scherer group and shakes hands with André, who's gone toward him.)

Prince Basile
Thanks. (Gesturing politely to Mortemart and to the generals, dodges a greeting from Berg and comes urgently to Countess Scherer.) Dear Annette! What a friend you are! To be present like this in our great sorrow.

Countess Scherer
Control yourself, my friend.

Bilibine
Yes, Prince—it has to be said, given the Count's age and how he's suffering his death will be a true deliverance for him and for others. (He moves away.)

Prince Basile
I am cruelly tested. My uncle, my benefactor. And it's the very moment that Anatole has chosen to cause a shocking scandal.

Countess Scherer
Yes, I know the vexing story. Besides, I don't like your Anatole. But your two other children are charming—Hippolyte—

Prince Basile
Hippolyte—let's talk about him. He's costing me, like his brother, 20,000 roubles a year. Because I'm doing for their education all that a father can do. And the result, two imbeciles. Hippolyte is a peaceful idiot, and Anatole is a turbulent idiot. That's the only difference between them.

Countess Scherer
You are very severe, but—at least, you will grant me that Helene—

Prince Basile
Yes, Helene—

Countess Scherer
Why, since her entry into society she's been the delight of our entire set. We find her gorgeous like the dawn.

Prince Basile
Yes, but she's been found gorgeous altogether too long. She's beginning to become a necessary addiction at every ball. She still has a sure dowry. And, according to the law—we and Catiche are the heirs.

Countess Scherer
Why, it's because your Helene is very proud, very difficult. Besides, she's right. She's a morsel fit for a king.

(A pause) I've got an idea! What would you say to Prince André. He's beginning the most brilliant career. And you know that the fortune of old Bolkonski....

Prince Basile
Fine. I abandon myself to you, dear friend. But still, Helene needs to be consulted about it.

Countess Scherer
Exactly where is the dear child?

Prince Basile
I wanted to get her out of here; this atmosphere is lugubrious. I sent her to the Rostovs.

Countess Scherer
The Rostovs. Why, I knew the Countess very well when she was young. I've never been able to understand why she decided to marry that stupid country-bumpkin.

Prince Basile
He's a very brave man.

Catiche
(Entering) He's a little drowsy.

(She goes to Countess Scherer. Anna Mikhailovna and Boris enter. General indifference)

Anna
And Pierre isn't here. After he promised me!

Catiche
(Noticing Anna and turning away.) Ah, that old shrew. She's come prowling around here again.

(Prince Basile, with an astonished air goes to Anna. Boris bows. The prince does not reply.)

Anna
Is it time? (Affirmative nod by Basile.) Ah! This is horrible. It's frightful to think of. (Presenting) My son, Boris, grandson of the Count, and thanks to you, lieutenant in the guards. He wants to thank you himself.

(Another deep bow by Boris, some disdain by The Count.)

Anna
Believe, Prince, that the heart of a mother, will never forget what you have done for us.

Prince Basile
Happy to have been able to be agreeable to you, my dear Anna Mikhailovna! (To Boris) Try to serve well, young man, and I will be satisfied. (He gestures with his hand dismissing him.)

Anna
My friend! Our benefactor! Just two more things. You are in good relations with General Koutouzov. If you would recommend Boris to him as an Aide de Camp? Then I'd be completely happy.

Prince Basile
That I cannot promise. You don't know how they besiege Koutouzov since he was appointed to his command. He told me himself. All the mothers in Moscow have joined together to give him their sons as Aides de Camp. Besides, this is not the place.

Anna
Excuse me! Could I see the patient? I want so much to thank him for all his kindness.

(Pointing to Boris and emphasizing.) For his grandson—and for me.

Catiche
(Turning, abruptly.) Now's not the time.

Anna
(Effusively) Ah, darling, I didn't recognize you. I came to place myself at your disposal to care for the dear patient. I imagine how much you have suffered. I won't ever leave you. (She takes off her hat and gloves, and installs herself in an armchair with a victorious pose, and by gesture invites Prince Basile to take a seat beside her. The Prince and Catiche move away without saying a word.)

Boris
Let's get out of here, Mama. All that you make me do results only in humiliations.

Anna
That's what we shall see, my dear. The will is going to say it all.

Boris
But why do you think the Count is leaving us something?

Anna
Oh—my child! He's so rich and we are so poor!

(Pierre enters, timidly, seemingly embarrassed and looking over his glasses without seeing anybody.)

Anna
(To Boris) Finally! There he is!

(Catiche rises violently. General reaction)

Pierre
Hello, cousin—you don't recognize me?

Catiche
I recognize you too well, too well!

Pierre
How's my father doing?

Catiche
Very badly. One would say that you've made it your business to cause him the most moral suffering imaginable.

Pierre
Can I see the Count?

Catiche
If you want to kill him right away, then go ahead.

Prince Basile
My dear boy, it's not a question of your behaving here as in Petersburg—you mustn't see him. His condition is most grave.

Pierre
But it's exactly because of that—

Catiche
Besides, at the moment he's sleeping—

Pierre
In that case, I'm going to wait in my apartment; when it's possible, you will indeed tell me.

Anna
(Excitedly) Why no, my friend, you mustn't go far off now.

André
(Coming forward and offering his hand to Pierre) Pierre

Pierre
André (They shake hands affectionately.) How long have you been in Moscow? How's your father?

André
He's fine, thanks. He still loves you a lot.

Countess Scherer
Well, Monsieur Pierre—don't you see me?

(To Catiche) No manners!

Pierre
Oh, Countess—I ask your pardon.

(He kisses her hand.—The group approaches and exchanges bows.)

Countess Scherer
Well, Monsieur Pierre, they are saying fine things about your conduct? Now, I hope—you are going to think of the future.

André
Indeed, my friend, have you finally decided something? Have you chosen? The Guards or Diplomacy?

Pierre
Neither, because in both cases it's war. Still, if they were fighting for liberty, I would understand and I would be the first to join the army.

André
If all made war from conviction there would be no more war.

Pierre
Now that would be beautiful! And that day will come. Yes, I feel it, universal peace is possible—but I cannot express it.

André
Replace the blood in our veins with water, and then nations will no longer battle between themselves.

Mortemart
Besides, so long as we have Monsieur Buonaparte, there won't be any peace possible.

Bilibine
Oh—Bonaparte, now that he's the son-in-law of His Majesty the Emperor of Austria—we can do him the grace of dropping the "U"—

Pierre
But Napoleon doesn't make war except to vanquish war, just as he served the Revolution only to vanquish anarchy.

Mortemart
Yes, he vanquished it by his violence, exile, executions. Society, I'm speaking of good French society, has been destroyed forever.

Pierre
But almost all the nobility has gone over to the side of Bonaparte.

Mortemart
That's what the Bonapartists say. It's difficult to know public opinion in France, now.

Pierre
It's Napoleon who said—I showed them the path to glory—they wanted no part of it. I opened my antechambers to them and they crowded in—in a rush.

Countess Scherer
Not all! There are good émigrés—true ones. The Vicomte de Mortemart (Presenting him with a gesture) The personal friend of Milord The Duke of Enghien

Pierre
I ask pardon of the Vicomte.

(Warning up) But the execution of The Duke was such a necessity of state that I see exactly the grandeur of Napoleon's soul—in not being afraid to take on himself the responsibility for this action.

Countess Scherer
My God! My God!

Bilibine
Colossal!

Pierre
And whatever anyone may say—Napoleon will forever remain for me the greatest man in the world.

Countess Scherer
No, Monsieur Pierre, there's only one great man in the world; it's our benefactor Alexander the First. I believe only in God and in the high destiny of our charming Emperor.

(Helene enters in an Empire gown, arms naked.)

Bilibine
As for me, I believe in the beauty of woman. (He bows)

Boris
(To his mother) Cristi! The beautiful girl!

Prince Basile
You've come back right on time my dear child. We are surrounded by friends and our sweet Countess was just speaking of you.

Helene
Oh—dear Anna Pavlovna!

Countess Scherer
Come, my dear Helene, let me embrace you.

Pierre
(Low to André) Isn't she beautiful?

André
Yes, an admirable statue!

Pierre
No, not a statue. She's living and trembling flesh. Look at her. She's sensuality itself. She's beautiful enough to cause harm.

André
What? Pierre?

Pierre
Yes, André, to you I can say it? It's a mad desire.

André
You've spoken to her of your love?

Pierre
She's shown me too much scorn. I don't dare. Me, without name, without fortune!

Countess Scherer
Well, Bolkonski! Yet another dispute. Come over to our side a bit.

Prince Basile
And now, my little one, you must indeed offer something to our friends—a cup of tea—in the gallery.

Helene
Willingly, Papa. You'll come help me, cousin?

Catiche
No, I must stay here.

Mortemart
Ah! I confess my weakness for that excellent Russian tea.

Helene
Then, gentlemen, would you indeed follow me? (Taking the arm of the Countess) Dear Countess! (They head out)

Pierre
(Bowing) Hello, Helene!

Helene
(Disdainfully) Ah! It's you? Hello!

Prince Basile
(To Anna) Dear Anna Mikhailovna aren't you coming?

Anna
No, dear Prince, Catiche is too worn out, I must second her.

(To Boris) You go on—As for me, I'm staying here.

(To Pierre, pushing Boris towards him) Count on me.

Pierre
(To Boris) Come, young man.

(They leave. Anna heads toward the Count's door)

Catiche
(Barring her way) Where are you going?

Anna
To see my benefactor.

Catiche
I told you already that's impossible; he cannot see strangers.

Anna
But my dear Catiche, I am not a stranger.

Prince Basile
Yes, Catiche, our dear Anna Mikhailovna is right. Let her enter.

Anna
Thanks.

(She goes in. Catiche wants to follow her—Basile holds her by the hand)

Basile
Stay put.

(Anna goes into the Count's room)

Prince Basile
I have to speak to you. In the end I have expedients. Not a minute to lose. In a moment like this one must think of everything—of the future, of ourselves! You know Catiche, that you and I are the sole heirs of the Count. (Reaction by Catiche) I know how painful it is for you to think of these things and to speak of them, but, my friend—

Catiche
I don't cease to pray God for one thing, cousin, that he absolve him, and to permit his beautiful soul to leave peacefully this—

Prince Basile
Yes, that's it, but still, it's a question you know it yourself, of this—Last winter the Count wrote a will by which he left all his wealth to Pierre, to the detriment of his loyal heirs—you and me.

Catiche
But he cannot leave anything to Pierre, he's a natural child.

Prince Basile
My dear, at the same time as this will—he wrote a letter to the Emperor—demanding the authority to adopt Pierre. Well—this letter has not yet been sent. We must know if it's been destroyed or not. The Emperor knows of its existence. Indeed as soon as everything is over—(Meaningfully) They will put seals on the Count's papers—an Aide de Camp of Rostopchine has remained expressly for that and the letter if it still exists will be sent to the Emperor with the will;— and the Count's wishes will surely be respected. Pierre—as a legitimate child will receive everything.

Catiche
And our share?

Prince Basile
(increasingly nervous) My poor Catiche, it's clear as day; once he becomes sole heir, our share will be zero. You can no longer remain unaware, my dear, as to whether the will or the letter have been destroyed or not. And if for a cause of some sort, they've been forgotten, you must learn where they are, and where to find them, because….

Catiche
This is unnecessary! You think all women are stupid. But I know quite well an illegitimate child cannot inherit. A bastard!

Prince Basile
But in that case he'll no longer be a bastard, but Count Bezhoukov. And one more time, I tell you, he'll get everything and nothing will remain to you save the consolation of having been virtuous and all that entails.

Catiche
I know that the will was written, but I also know it's worthless.

Prince Basile
My dear Princess Catherine, now's not the time to exchange unpleasant words. I am speaking to you as a good relative, of your own interests. I repeat to you for the tenth time—if the letter is delivered to the Emperor—Pierre will get everything, and you, my little pigeon, nothing at all, and that goes for me, too. These are the very words of our lawyer—advisor.

Catiche
Ah—That would be nice! Now, that's his gratitude for those who have sacrificed everything for him! But as for me, I don't need it!

Prince Basile
Yes, but you are not alone.

Catiche
Yes, I'd forgotten that, except for the blackest ingratitude I cannot expect anything from this house.

Prince Basile
Yes or no, do you know where the will is? I entreat you by Christ!

Catiche
Now, I understand everything. I know who's plotting intrigues.

Prince Basile
It's not a question of that.

Catiche
It's your protégée, your darling Princess Anna Mikhailovna, who I wouldn't have as a chamber maid. That villainous woman! That horrible Megara!

Prince Basile
Time's wasting!

Catiche
Don't talk to me about it. Last winter she got herself introduced here, and then the Count wrote that nasty that cursed paper. I thought that this document signified nothing.

Prince Basile
Here we go! At last. But why didn't you tell me anything about it?

Catiche
He has it stuck under his pillow in a portfolio in mosaic—That's where the letter and the will are.

Anna
(Entering on the word portfolio) Ah.

(She casts a suspicious look at Catiche and Prince Basile)

Catiche
(Uneasily) What's wrong.?

Prince Basile
The Count.

Anna
He's asking to see Pierre.

Catiche
That's not true. He can no longer speak.

Anna
No—but he indicated with a look at the portrait of his son and I understood his wish.

Prince Basile
That's fine, go find him, my good Anna Mikhailovna. (She leaves by the left)

Prince Basile
And now do what you have to do.

Catiche
What?

Prince Basile
The portfolio.

Catiche
It's a sacrilege.

Prince Basile
No, it's your duty. You must avert the Count's sin of dying and despoiling his heirs designated by the law and by God.

Catiche
But his last will?

Count Basile
They are not his last will. They are the will of Anna Mikhailovna, the horrible Megara.

Catiche
I'm going there. But the nurse.

Prince Basile
Send her away—Go quickly. As for me I'm keeping watch.

(Catiche goes into the Count's room)

(Prince Basile holds the Count's door, half open and listens. At this moment a priest enters by another door, he's carrying a gold cross and The Evangelist, followed by a deacon and two children of the choir, carrying sacred objects and lit candles. Prince Basile recoils and—the Count's door opens—Catiche emerges holding the mosaic portfolio)

Catiche
(Emerging—and extending the portfolio to Prince Basile) Here it is!

(At the sight of the clergy she instinctively hides the portfolio behind her—The priest, as he nears Catiche, extends the cross to her which she kisses—Following the clergy the people of the household including the lady and the Major Domo enter the Count's room. Anna Mikhailovna enters with Pierre and observes Catiche hiding the portfolio)

Anna
(To Pierre) Courage, courage, my friend. Divine goodness is inexhaustible. Come!

Prince Basile
(To Countess Scherer who enters with André, Berg and General Dokhtourov) Come my friends, join your prayers to ours. The ceremony of Extreme Unction is about to begin.

(They go into the room with Prince Basile. The doors remain open and the backs of those present holding candles can be seen Catiche intends to follow but she is stopped by Anna Mikhailovna. During the following prayers are said in the room of the dying man)

Anna
(Low) Give me the portfolio.

Catiche
(Low) What? What portfolio?

Anna
The one you've got—with the last will in it.

Catiche
I don't know even what's in it. All I know is the real will is in his desk.

(She wants to go in. Anna bars her way and seizes the portfolio)

Anna
But I know, my dear sweet Princess; I entreat you.

Catiche
(Trying to hold the portfolio) Intriguer!—Who's making scenes in the doorway of a dying man.

Anna
Look, give it to me.

Catiche
Remember, you will be responsible for all the consequences. You don't know what you are doing.

(The portfolio slips from Catiche's hands and Anna Mikhailovna grabs it)

Anna
Ah, at last.

Catiche
Thief.

(At this moment, the singing stops. A moment of absolute silence. After that whispering. A great reaction takes place)

Catiche
Rejoice now! You were waiting for this.

(She goes into the room to Basile as he leaves followed by Pierre) She snatched it from me.

Basile
(Controlling his reaction, then turning towards Pierre in the most friendly way) Ah, my friend—how we sin, how we lie, and all this—why? Everything ends in death, everything. Death is terrible.

Anna
How prompt it was. Try to cry, nothing eases like tears.

An Aide de Camp from the Governor
(Entering from the right to Prince Basile) Excellency, in the name of His Majesty the Emperor—I've come to put seals on the papers of Count Bezhoukov.

Anna
Begin, officer, with this portfolio—It contains the last will of the deceased.

Prince Basile
Yes, sir, do your duty. You'll be given all the keys, Captain.

(The officer leaves followed by the Major Domo. To Pierre) My dear child, it's a great loss for all of us. But God will sustain you. You are young—and you will bear worthily the responsibility of a great name and an immense fortune.

Pierre
What do you mean?

Prince Basile
I am sure of not being mistaken when I tell you that the Count by his will, which besides answering all our wishes makes you heir to all his wealth and title as Count Bezhoukov—

Berg
(To André) My dear Prince, shall I dare already to ask you for a service.

André
Gladly, what?

Berg
Present me again to Count Bezhoukov—

André
In a moment.

Anna
(To Pierre, low) My dear friend, perhaps later I will tell you what would have happened if I hadn't been here, God knows—You know my uncle promised me not to forget Boris.

(Pointing to her son) I hope, my dear, you will fulfill the desire of your father.

Pierre
Count on me, my dear Anna Mikhailovna.

Countess Scherer
Well, my dear. I hope that we will remain friends as before, and that Count Bezhoukov won't forget the affection that old Countess Scherer had for Monsieur Pierre

Pierre
Countess I am touched, believe—

Countess Scherer
Helene, you aren't saying anything to your cousin.

Helene
My poor Pierre.

Prince Basile
You no longer have a father but a family remains to you, my child. Embrace your cousin.

Countess Scherer
(To Basile) These children are charming, Bolkonski was good, but Countess Bezhoukov is even better!

Pierre
And you, André—are you abandoning me?

André
You no longer need me, you have so many friends.

Pierre
I know there's only one on whom I can actually count.

(They shake hands affectionately)

Old Woman
(To Boris) It's painful, but all this is for the good; it elevates the soul to see men like the old Count and his worthy son and all these relatives so tenderly united.

(To Pierre) But you are standing. Excellency, permit me to offer you my armchair.

Pierre
(Vexed) Oh, Madame!

(He sits and drops his handkerchief. Berg rushes to pick it up)

Pierre
(Vexed) Oh, Captain!

Berg
Not yet, Excellency. Lieutenant Berg of the Preobrajensky Regiment.

Major Domo
(To Pierre) Excellency, prayers for the repose of the soul of Count Cyril Vladimirovitch Bezhoukov are going to begin.

(The door of the deceased's room open. Everyone heads there crossing themselves. A religious chant can be heard)

Man in Black
(Entering) And now?

Major Domo
Now you can enter.

(The curtain falls slowly)

CURTAIN

ACT II

Scene 2

Petersburg, in the palace of Anna Pavlovna Scherer. A waiting salon—to the left a large dance salon—in the back a gallery. Door to the right giving on an antechamber. At the right a large chimney. In a corner near the entry an icon. Sumptuous furniture in the Louis XVI style. All along the wall golden chairs. On the wall, pictures by eighteenth-century masters.

The Rostov family is seated on the right, the Countess, Anna Mikhailovna, Natasha Sonia, and young Petia behind the chair of Countess Rostov.

The salon is brilliantly lit. Before the rise of the curtain very lively dance music can be heard.

At rise there are several couples dancing, brilliant officers and ladies in décolleté—among them are Prince André with Julie Kouraguine, Berg with his fiancée, Vera Rostov; Anatole Kouraguine, Dolokhov, Nesvitzki and Mortemart. After several tours the dancers disperse into other salons. The music stops.

Julie Kouraguine
(To André leading him back to large salon) Who's that picture of a family? Some provincial relatives of our dear hostess?

André
Of Countess Scherer? Oh, no, they are good Muscovites. They are the family of our new Marshall of the Nobility, Count Rostov.

(They go back to the dance room with other couples who disperse laughing)

Natasha
(Pointing out André to her mother as he moves away with Julie) Look at that, Mama! It's Bolkonski. You recall, he spent the night at our home in Otradnoie.

Anna Mikhailovna
Ah, you know him? I detest him. He's ruling the roost now. A pride without limits. He's like his father.

Petia
He has a beautiful uniform, but not as beautiful as my brother Nicholas's—right, Sonia?

Sonia
(Blushing) Oh—I don't know about uniforms.

Natasha
Look you there. Yes, we know that with Nikolenka it's not the uniform but the officer that you like.

Sonia
Oh, Natasha, you are the most insupportable of cousins—

Natasha
And you will be the most adorable of sisters-in-law.

Anna Mikhailovna
What a shame he didn't come with you to Petersburg, your Nicholas.

Countess Rostov
But where is your Boris? The children are counting on him for a dance.

Anna Mikhailovna
Since I had obtained his nomination with General Dokhtourov—

Countess Rostov
Oh—you are an admirable mother.

Anna Mikhailovna
I have no great merit. It's not for nothing I had such a lucky role in the affairs of the Bezhoukov family. Since then, Prince Basile refuses me nothing. He spoke to General Dokhtourov on whom all nominations depend at the moment. But my poor Boris is terribly taken. This very evening he was called to the palace. He

told me he'd come very late if he comes at all. It seems great events are in preparation.

Natasha
I'm vexed without Boris. The greatest event is my first ball. It's not nice of him. But we will do very well without him, won't we, my little cousin?

Sonia
But Berg also promised to present cavaliers to us and get us dances.

Natasha
Oh, my little Sonia! I entreat you, no more of Berg and his cavaliers. I leave them to Vera. (The opening measures of a dance can be heard) Quick, quick, Mama! Do I look okay? Ah, this ribbon! Sonia I beg you.

(Sonia arranges her hair) Ah, now, I believe that we can show ourselves.

Sonia
You are ravishing.

(Dancers pass in the gallery among them Anatole Kouraguine and a lady)

Natasha
(Stopping) Ah, now there's a cavalier who suits me.

Anna Mikhailovna
It's that good-for-nothing Anatole, Helene's brother—

Petia
Oh, auntie, today she likes all the beaux—

(To Natasha) It's true—you are in love with everybody. (The girls leave)

Anna Mikhailovna
But what's become of your husband? He's abandoning us.

Countess Rostov
Ely? He's busy dancing. He's intoxicated by the atmosphere of your Petersburg. But, as for me, I feel completely out of place here. And if it weren't for the children—I was hoping, at least, to meet our friend Pierre Bezhoukov and we haven't seen him yet.

Anna Mikhailovna
Oh—you needn't worry—he will come. Not for his pleasure, but to accompany his wife—now the Queen of Petersburg—

Countess
Isn't that a pleasure for him? He was so happy to marry his cousin Helene.

Anna Mikhailovna
Oh, my darling, at present, he's very unhappy. If what they say of him is true, it's horrible. And to think that we were so overjoyed for his happiness! A soul so superior, so celestial, this young Bezhoukov. He's been so nice to my Boris. So, as far as possible. I will try to console him.

Countess Rostov
Why, what's the matter?

Anna Mikhailovna
They say the Grand Duke is mad about her. The Austrian ambassador pays her assiduous court. They also speak of Doctor Metvier. But it's Captain Dolokhov who has definitively compromised her. She made him her protégé, invited him to her home in Petersburg. And there you have it. This rake—(Indulgent smile) Finally, here's our dear Count.

Countess Scherer
(Entering) Dear friend I am bringing you back your husband.

Countess Rostov
And a husband rejuvenated by twenty years! What a fancy ball!

Countess Scherer
A little informal dance party. Still, I'm arranging an agreeable surprise for you!

Anna Mikhailovna
A surprise! What is it?

Countess
The celebrated Mademoiselle George will come to declaim something for us.

Countess Rostov
Oh! And as for me I've never heard her.

Countess
It's exactly as our great friend Maria Dmitrievna was telling me just now, but she added she won't stay long.

Countess Rostov
What, Maria Dmitrievna is here?

Countess Scherer
Yes, we've got the terrible dragon. What an admirable woman. And so amusing with her bluntness.

Countess Rostov
I love her so much.

Countess Scherer
The whole world loves her. And it's so beautiful that she always speaks the truth. Well? And your children.

Countess Rostov
They went into the larger room.

Countess Scherer
Then, dear friend let's go see them. They are charming!

(They head to the large salon)

Bilibine
Ah, Countess, we're looking for a refuge. The dancers are chasing us out of every place.

(The Countess Rostov and Anna Mikhailovna go into the neighboring salon after giving the Countess Scherer a sign, they are leaving her to her duties as hostess.)

Countess Scherer
Come over here, gentlemen. I will be enchanted to have you for a bit in my little corner.

(To Hippolyte) But you, my dear Hippolyte, why aren't you dancing?

Hippolyte
(With a noisy laugh) Now that I'm in diplomacy.

Bilibine
You are afraid of compromising the European balance of power.

Prince Basile
I've never seen a ball more gay than yours, my dear Annette. What spirit in all this youth.

Bilibine
While it lasts.

Countess Scherer
What, my dear Bilibine—could you have learned something serious?

Bilibine
The situation is very delicate. There can be an unavoidable catastrophe at any moment. Napoleon has reached the extreme limit of our territory—and of our patience. Here he is on the shore of the Niemen. If he crosses the river there's nothing more to do except let the cannons speak.

Countess Scherer
What a calamity! In any case if some catastrophe occurs we will know of it before all the rest. Tonight, there are councils being held in the palace of the Aide de Camp of General Balaschov, Prince Boris Droubetzkoi has promised to come bring me news of it however late he may be.

Bilibine
Anyway Bonaparte acts with Europe as with a conquered ship; for many months now all his actions have been only a continual provocation. This odious blockade—

Countess Scherer
Ah, the Continental blockade! That's not the worst. Napoleon forbids us to purchase anything whatever from England. But how does this Irish lace seem to you? No, what is abominable is the uncle of our charming Emperor has been driven from his duchy.

Prince Basile
I read a protest over that affair and I was astonished by the bad wording of the note.

Count Rostov
The wording of the note doesn't matter if the contents were strong.

Bilibine
My dear Count, with our 500,000 men army it would be easy to have a fine style.

Countess Scherer
You've heard of the incident of the military review?

Count Rostov
What?

Countess Scherer
His Majesty drew the attention of the French Ambassador to the order of precedence in the grand regiments—and the Ambassador Count Lauriston negligently replied that in France no one paid attention to such trifles.

Count Rostov
And what did the Emperor say?

Countess Scherer
His Majesty didn't deign to reply, but at the review that followed he did not address a single word to His Excellency the French Ambassador.

General Dokhtourov
A nice lesson! At least the French will know that the Russians are not afraid of war.

Prince Basile
Oh, my dear general, are we able to make war against the French? Look at our youth, look at our ladies. Our Gods are the French—our heavenly realm is Paris. We think French thoughts, our feelings are French, a French theater costs us more than an army corps. And who is our great doctor? Metvier—before whom all our ladies drag themselves. On their knees—because he is French.

General Dokhtourov
You are right, Prince, when I look at our youth, I'm seized with the desire to steal from the museums the old baton of Peter the Great and to break their heads on all sides—the Russian way! Then we'd have an end to all these stupidities.

(Pierre, Anatole and Helene enter)

Countess Scherer
Finally, dear friends, you are here—we were despairing

Pierre
We beg your pardon, Countess—we were forced to go to make an appearance at the Austrian Embassy. (Dokhtourov, Rostov, Bilibine surround Helene)

Dolokhov
The next waltz, dear Countess.

Helene
Gladly, Captain.

Pierre
But for nothing in the world would we have missed your party. Right, my dear, Helene?

Helene
(Low to Dolokhov) I need to talk to you.

Anatole
(Going to Pierre who is going to Helene) My dear brother-in-law—I absolutely need 3,000 roubles.

Pierre
But last Saturday you received your monthly salary.

Anatole
Yes, but Dolokhov had made a clean sweep of me on the side.

Pierre
(Distracted, observing his wife) Well, well, wait till tomorrow.

Anatole
Understood. (He leaves)

Prince Basile
My dear Pierre, I know this isn't the place, but since I've met you, and I've taken up your interests from pure charity, I've received from the domain of Riazan 40,000 roubles. I'm keeping them. We'll count them later?

Pierre
(Still distracted) That's fine, thanks.

Prince Basile
There's nothing to thank me for, my dear—I'm doing it for myself, for my conscience.

(The sounds of a waltz. Countess Scherer, Dokhtourov, Rostov and Bilibine head toward the exit)

Helene
(To Dolokhov) Careful, he's suspicious.

Dolokhov
Very stupid. And then, so much the worse for him.

Pierre
Helene, a word.

Helene
What do you want with me?

Pierre
I beg you don't dance this waltz.

Helene
(Ironically) Do you want to dance it with me? You're only a fool!

(To Dolokhov) Your arm, Captain.

(They leave. A violent reaction by Pierre to follow the group, but at this moment André arrives to detain him)

Countess Scherer
You got here apropos, Prince Count Bezhoukov was waiting for you.

(All leave except André and Pierre)

André
(Holding Pierre back) What's wrong my friend? You seem overwhelmed.

Pierre
I will kill him!

André
Who?

Pierre
That man. How did I end up like this? Oh—to allow myself to be caught so!

André
But you loved her, your beautiful cousin?

Pierre
No, I didn't love her! It's her body I wanted. What shame! even at my father's death bed I had this obsession with it, I saw her naked under her gray dress. Oh cursed be the day I told her "I love you!" I was deceiving her as I deceived myself. And yet, how many times have I been proud of her, proud of her majestic beauty, proud of her worldly tact, of a house where she received all Petersburg! Often I thought that I didn't understand her, I reproached myself for not discovering what was under this perpetual calm, this self containment, this absence of passion and desires. But the solution is contained in this terrible word: debauched.

André
Debauched! Helene. She's a woman like the others, more beautiful, that's all. What do you complain of? What, you Pierre, with all your wit, and your heart, you don't know what woman are in general! My father's right—egoism, ambition, stupidity, nullity in everything, and as you say yourself, debauched. There they are—when they show themselves such as they are. And it's for a woman that you torture yourself so.

Pierre
But, my friend, these are some sufferings that one cannot master. My life, for the last two years has been a Calvary. I tried not to see, not to hear. But one would have said she herself wanted to enlighten me through the strength of her scorn. If her father, jokingly excited her jealousy, she replied with a tranquil smile "That she wasn't so naive as to be jealous. Let him do what he wants", she said. Once, I asked her if she didn't hope to be a mother, she replied with a scornful laugh she wasn't stupid enough to want children and that with me—she couldn't have them.

André
But those are only hurtful words!

Pierre
If it were only words. But her attitude with all men who come to my home, all, even to her brother—Anatole who comes to her to borrow money and kisses her naked shoulders—and now, this Dolokhov—

André
Dolokhov? That cynical puppet. You aren't going to take him seriously?

Pierre
I'm actually forced to. Again this morning, I received an anonymous letter in which I'm told I see poorly through my glasses and that his relations with my wife are not a secret, except to me.

André
Look where you are! Anonymous letters.

Pierre
This told the truth. I feel it, I know it—and I will kill him.

Berg
(To André) Ah, my dear Prince, my respects.

(To Pierre) Excellency, I am really happy to meet you.

Pierre
Sir—Ah, yes—Lieutenant Berg.

Berg
No, my dear Count, Captain Berg of the Preobrajensky Regiment.

Pierre
Enchanted (Starts to leave)

Berg
Excuse me, dear Count. I have a prayer to address you.

André
(To Pierre) You will rejoin me.

Pierre
(Nervously) No, stay. We'll leave to together. Speak quickly, Captain. How can I be useful to you?

Berg
You see, Excellency, I am getting married.

Pierre
Ah—

Berg
You see, I calculated everything, because I didn't get married without considering, that's for sure, and if it was disadvantageous—But now my father and mother are very much at their ease; I've installed them in a small property on the Baltic and for myself, I will be able to live in Petersburg with my savings, my wife's fortune and my salary one could really live.

André
Compliments.

Berg
It goes without saying that it's necessary to be exact and virtuous. And the important thing is a nice young girl, respectful and who loves me.

Pierre
And who is this incomparable person?

Berg
Miss Vera Rostov, the daughter of Count Rostov.

Pierre
Ah, Vera. I congratulate you. she is indeed charming. But I didn't know anything.

Berg
It was decided only yesterday. And me, too, I love her because she has a reasonable deposition and she is very nice. Ah, I wouldn't say as much of her younger sister, Natasha she has a disagreeable personality without wit, in the end, something you know, unpleasant. While my fiancée….

Pierre
But in what way can I be useful to you?

Berg
I want to ask you, Excellency, to do me the great honor of being my witness.

Pierre
Gladly, Captain, especially as I am a great friend of the Rostov family. And now, excuse me.

(To André) Let's go, André.

(They leave)

Berg
(To Count Rostov who enters) Ah, my dear father-in-law, I have good news to announce to you! Count Bezhoukov has agreed to be my witness.

Count Rostov
Ah, I'm very pleased about that. It will be a beautiful marriage.

Natasha
(Entering vexed) I've had enough of it; let's leave, Mama.

Count Rostov
What's the matter with you, my darling?

Natasha
(Throwing herself into his arms) Ah, Papa—I will cry over it. And I was having such a great party! No one thought of inviting me. If they by chance deigned to look at me right away they seemed to be saying, "Ah, it's not she" "In that case it's not worth the trouble!" No, no, it's not possible, they must realize that I want to dance, that I dance well and that it would be great fun to dance with me.

Vera
Natasha—do you know what Berg's told me? Our marriage.

Natasha
Ah, no, my darling Vera, no family conversations here.

Count Rostov
(Noticing Maria Dmitrievna) Heavens! Why, it's Maria Dmitrievna.

Maria Dmitrievna
Herself. Ah, old sinner. Happy to see you.

(To Countess) And you, to hug you, my dear old friend!

(To Count) Huh?—It's less amusing than hunting? But, what do you want, my little father, when wings sprout on these birds, it's necessary that their old fathers return to the ball.

(To Natasha) Well, my Cossack has nothing to say. You are making a face. Why she's crying—my word.

Countess Rostov
She's desolate because so far no one's invited her to dance.

Maria Dmitrievna
Why that's revolting! My poor little hobgoblin! Ah, indeed. Do they all have their eyes in their pockets?

Natasha
Oh, god-mother-how miserable I am (Noticing Pierre who's passing) Ah—look, Count Bezhoukov.

Maria Dmitrievna
At least his wife isn't with him? But for that I'd run off.

Pierre
(Entering) Ah! Maria Dmitrievna, my respects.

Maria Dmitrievna
Hello, my nice booby.

Pierre
(Turning) You, my dear Natasha?

(To Count Rostov) Why your daughter is ravishing!

Natasha
You think so? Well others are not of your opinion. No one has asked me.

Pierre
Oh—I am unforgivable! But I'm going to bring you a cavalier, the best dance in the court—immediately.

Maria Dmitrievna
Well—now that you are settled and that I've seen you all—I'm going to put myself to bed. In my house in Moscow I'd have gone to bed long ago. Goodbye, friends—You must bring me my little Cossack tomorrow—She will tell me about her conquests.

(She leaves)

Pierre
(Seeing André chattering with someone) André, listen. I have a protégée, young Miss Rostov.

André
Ah—the disagreeable little lady of whom Berg was speaking.

Natasha
Mama, look. He's speaking to Pierre Bolkonski.

Pierre
She's delightful. You must dance with her.

André
At your orders.

Natasha
Mama, he's coming. (Aside) Oh—I've been waiting for you for a long time.

Pierre
(Returning with André) Dear Countess, allow me to present my friend to you—Prince André Bolkonski.

Countess Rostov
Enchanted, Prince. Permit me, in my turn to present my daughter.

(Waltz music)

André
Miss, would you do me the honor of granting me this waltz?

Natasha
With pleasure, Prince.

Countess Rostov
(To Pierre) How likable your friend is!

Pierre
Ah, he's a superior man in every respect. Oh, but as for me, how clumsy I am, my friends. I was forgetting to congratulate you.

Count Rostov
It's our turn.

Vera
(To Berg) Well, my friend—shall we dance?

Berg
In a minute, my darling—Go with the Countess—I need to speak briefly with your father.

(The Countess and Vera leave)

Berg
A couple things, my dear father-in-law. You are leaving tomorrow, and before you do I'd like to have your response. You would agree, Count, that if I allowed myself to marry without having the means to take care of my wife in a suitable way, I would be acting in a cowardly fashion. That's why I beg you to tell me exactly what Vera's dowry will be?

Count Rostov
It pleases me that you don't engage yourself lightly. You will be satisfied.

Berg
(Smiling agreeably) No, Papa—I would like a figure, without which you understand, I would be forced to—

Count Rostov
Well, my son, I will give you a note payable to order—for 80,000 roubles. Are you satisfied? I hope so. And now let's go watch the young folks dance.

Berg
(Kissing his shoulder) I am indeed grateful to you, but these notes—

(They leave)

Natasha
(Coming with André) I'm quite sure I left it here.

(The music starts again)

André
Wait. Here it is.

(He takes a fan from a console and gives it to Natasha)

Natasha
Thanks. And now let's return quickly.

André
You don't want to stay here a bit—to rest a little?

Natasha
With pleasure. But it's not because I'm tired. You waltz admirably. You are truly the best dancer of the court. (Laughs)

André
What's this joke?

Natasha
It was Count Bezhoukov who described you thus. (She laughs)

André
You are making fun of me. But who cares, I love your laughter so never mind. It's a joy for me to hear it again.

Natasha
What do you mean, again?

André
Yes, I've already heard it. It was at Otradnoie, at your father's home. As my carriage was in the avenue I saw a young girl with black hair and black eyes. She was running on the road but seeing me she fled laughing in whoops.

Natasha
What! You remember that?

André
And many other things as well.

Natasha
What, for example?

André
A lovely conversation by moonlight.

Natasha
By moonlight?

André
The night that your father gave me hospitality was splendid. So beautiful that I didn't think of sleeping. I had opened my window. Two young girls were chatting in the garden—amusing themselves a bit at the expense of a stranger.

Natasha
Oh—Sir—it wasn't me.

André
Oh—yes, Miss. I indeed recognized the voice of a charming child.

Natasha
Oh—you are making me blush!

André
Don't blush, Miss; it was delicious and I envied your youthful joy. You seemed to be so happy.

Natasha
(Dumbly) I am—now!

Sonia
(Entering) Natasha! Natasha! It's your turn. (Anatole and Julie are with her)

Natasha
I beg your pardon. I would have loved to remain, but you see, they are calling me.

André
(Aside) If she goes to her cousin first, she will be my wife.

(Natasha goes toward her cousin takes her hand and leaves laughing with her) What stupidities we get in our head from time to time.

Pierre
(Entering) You are alone? Oh, what a funny look. Now it's my turn to ask you—what's wrong with you?

André
I'm crazy. Do you know what I was thinking when you entered? Of marrying Natasha Rostov. Certainly, I won't do it, but this young girl is so charming, there's so much original about her, so much youthful freshness—a real rarity in our world—she won't dance here more than a month and she'll be married.

Pierre
You are right. That young girl is such a treasure, such— Dear friend, don't consider, don't doubt—get married. I'm convinced there won't be a happier man than you.

André
(Laughing) Look, Pierre, look. You indeed know my opinion about women and marriage; the laughter from Miss Natasha doesn't dazzle sufficiently to change it.

Pierre
That's a big shame!

Berg
(Entering with Vera) Pardon me for interrupting you, but I wanted to have the honor, Prince, of presenting my future wife to you, Countess Vera Rostov.

André
Ah, Miss I am happy to congratulate the Captain. I was just now hearing my friend Pierre praising you and I see it is deserved.

Vera
(Bowing) Oh! Prince. But Count Bezhoukov has always spoiled us.

Pierre
Ah, it's because I'm friends with all the Rostov children . And whatever makes them happy rejoices me. You know that Natasha with her first waltz caused a sensation.

Vera
Oh—nothing surprising about that. She's used to success, my little sister. No young girl has been more courted than she. But until now no one made her weep—

André
Truly?

Pierre
Well—someone will please her and he will be the happiest of men.

Vera
Oh, certainly. Natasha is adorable but just on account of her flighty excitable character—one can wonder if she'll know how to remain faithful to her attachments, if like other women she can love a man, and keep faith with him entirely—which is, I believe, true love. What do you think about it—Count?

Pierre
As for me, I am sure of my little Natasha.

André
For my part, I've noticed that the less a woman pleases, the more faithful she is.

Vera
How true that is, Prince. And it must be confessed that Natasha is very sensitive to praise.

(To Pierre) You know, Count, between ourselves, our charming cousin Boris was very, very far into the land of tenderness. (Prince André scowls) But he must have spoken to you of his childhood love of Natasha.

André
Ah—he had a childhood love?

Vera
Yes—You know between cousins—intimacy sometimes leads to love. Cousinhood is a dangerous neighborhood, right?

André
(Nervously) Ah—no question. It's fatal. And I am sure that your friend Pierre with his cousin Catiche.

(A loud burst of applause)

Berg
Ah, it's Mademoiselle Georges, my dear Vera, we ought to hear her. An opportunity like this is not to be missed (Hastily bowing) Gentlemen.

André
Miss.

Pierre
Captain.

André
Well—there's your treasure, Natasha!

Pierre
But that was childishness, and once married—

André
Oh, all that is without importance and besides, the moment is singularly chosen to think of marriage. Aren't we on the eve of war, of the greatest war, perhaps, that history will ever speak of? Finally, we are going to be able to shake off the yoke under which Bonaparte holds all Europe and deliver our country to its glorious destiny.

Pierre
Then the war's going to start again? One's going to see this event contrary to reason and human nature take place. Millions of men are going to commit against each other a considerable quantity of crimes, of betrayals, of thefts, of fires, of murders, that the annals of all the tribunals in the world from all past countries don't contain! And that's what you call returning to the fatherland it's glorious destiny.

André
No, my dear friend, let's not discuss this subject where we will never be in agreement. For you, war is only a series of abominable crimes. For me war is holy in that it leads men to all great and noble feelings: honor, disinterestedness , virtue, courage—

Pierre
There you go—honor, virtue, courage.

Dolokhov
Surely it's a pleasure, it's a pleasure to dig in one's spurs into the belly on one's mare and to charge, sabers out, a fine galloping charge—but it's a much greater pleasure to hold a beautiful creature pressed against one's breast and to make her whirl to the point of intoxication.

Nesvitzki
And tonight beautiful women are not lacking.

Dolokhov
But there's only one here who counts for me.

Pierre
(To André) You hear him.

Dolokhov
Ah, this good Pierre. One amuses oneself a bit.

(To André) Excuse me, Prince, but Pierre and I —we are all comrades. We have so many things in common. And you know it's always necessary to coddle the husbands of pretty women.

André
I believe, Captain, you are a bit too gay. Leave my friend Pierre in peace.

Dolokhov
Me. But I haven't drunk anything. I even have a great thirst (to a valet with a platter of caps) Ah, champagne's coming at the right moment. (All take a cup, Dolokhov raises his) And now, gentlemen, to the health of pretty ladies (going to Pierre) To the health of pretty ladies—and their lovers.

Pierre
(Knocking his glass from his hand) You—you are a coward.

Dolokhov
A provocation. Ah, now that's what I love! Nesvitzki, I am counting on you.

(Helen, appears at the back—to Pierre) Till tomorrow at Iles!

(To Helene) Countess, I kiss your hand.

André
(Shaking Pierre's hand) You can count on me.

(He leaves with Nesvitzki and Anatole)

Helene
What is it this time? What have you done? I'm asking you!

Pierre
What? Me?

Helene
Ah!—You want to show yourself brave! Well—answer! What's this duel signify? What do you want to prove? What! I'm asking you? If you don't reply, then as for me, I will tell you. You believe everything they tell you. They told you Dolokhov was my lover and you believed it! Well! What have you proved by this provocation? That you're a fool! Everybody knows that? Where's all this leading? To my becoming the subject of the laughter all Petersburg. Everyone will say that you, being drunk, provoked a duel with a man you have no reason to be jealous of—and who is better than you in every respect.

Pierre
Don't speak to me like this, I beg you—! This is not the time.

Helene
Why shouldn't I speak? I can say, and I will say boldly to everyone that there are few women who, with a husband like you wouldn't take a lover. Well, as for me, I didn't do it.

Pierre
(Choked) Enough! Enough! Let's separate.

Helene
Separate? Why, that's all I ask for! If you think you can frighten me with that—

Pierre
Shut up, shut up!

Helene
On the condition, you understand that you abandon your fortune to me. I've earned it.

Pierre
(Hurling himself on her) I will kill you, slut.

(Helene flees, shocked)

André
(Returning) Everything's agreed. You will fight tomorrow morning with pistols.

Pierre
Fine.

André
Fine! You're going to try to kill a man, and there's the application of your fine theories.

Berg
(Entering, smiling to Pierre) Me, again, Excellency. I'm abusing truly, but I've just noticed General Dokhtourov, do I dare to ask you to present me—you understand on the occasion of my marriage.

Pierre
Fine, fine.

Anna Mikhailovna
(Entering with Boris) But when are you leaving….

Boris
This very night, Mama—

Countess Scherer
(Followed by all the characters) Finally now—here's our captain. Well you are bringing us news?

Boris
Very grave news, Madame. Napoleon has crossed the Niemen.

(General reaction)

All
Ah—

André
He dared!

Boris
His troops, pushing back our Cossacks, have crossed the Russian frontier.

Count Rostov
The sacred soil of the Fatherland—

Nesvitzki
...Outraging the Imperial Majesty.

Bilibine
Alea jacta est (The die is cast).

Prince Basile
It's war!

All
Yes, yes, war—

Dolokhov
Finally—were going to battle someone worth the trouble.

Countess Scherer
But what did His Majesty say?

Boris
It was General Balaschov who brought the news to the Emperor—and His Majesty with the emotion of an offended man uttered these words: "To enter Russia without a declaration of

war. I'll never be satisfied while a single enemy remains on my soil."

Count Rostov
It's the voice of the Fatherland .

All
Long live our father, The Tsar.

Count Rostov
We will all leave. We will sacrifice everything for Russia. We will give up our peasants, our wealth—and ourselves.

And Old General
(Leaning on his cane) I've still got enough life in me to give it for my Emperor.

Petia
Father, allow me to go rejoin my brother in the army.

Bilibine
(To Dokhtourov) You see the old baton of Peter the Great remains in our museum. The French fashion is passé!

All
Yes, yes—down with the foreigner.

Boris
But His Majesty wanted to place everything in good order on his side. He ordered General Balaschov to deliver a letter to Napoleon in which—reminding him with firmness and moderation, how his aggression lacks justification—and leaving him the master of avoiding the calamites a new war will bring to humanity and declaring himself ready to negotiate—

All
Negotiate!

Boris
On condition that Napoleon withdraw his troops from Russian territory.

All
Hurrah!

Boris
And His Majesty gave the explicit order to General Balaschov to repeat to Napoleon these words exactly: "I will never agree to negotiate so long as a single French soldier remains in Russian territory."

All
(In an enflamed reaction of enthusiasm while the Hymn bursts out): "Be Glorious, Emperor Alexander!" Long live the Emperor! Long live Russia!

CURTAIN

ACT II

Scene 3

Vilna

A large office in the Palace of the Governor of Vilna. Doors on all sides and at the back. The secretary seated at a large table writing at the dictation of Napoleon, who strides back and forth.

Napoleon
(Dictating) To Count Montalivet, Minister of the Interior. Witness my displeasure to Monsieur de Voyer d' Argenson, prefect of Deux-Nethes for the ridiculous conduct which he displayed at last Sunday's ceremony. Instead of going to take the general to his home, to accompany him—he went directly to the church and then made a scene worthy of the boulevard.

(An officer enters then stops and remains in the doorway in a military posture)

What's this? What's wrong?

Officer
Sire, the extraordinary envoy of the Emperor of Russia, General Balaschov, to whom you indeed wanted to set an audience for, is awaiting Your Majesty's orders.

Napoleon
Fine. Beg the General to wait. I am going to receive him in a moment.

(The Officer leaves; to the Secretary) Let's resume "Make known to this prefect that he must have some respect for a General, ,mutilated on the battlefield, and charged with a command as important as that of Anvers. That it's not proper to disturb the harmony between the civil and military authority, in any country, and especially in France where the military has earned the right not to be scorned and mistreated.

(Napoleon goes to the table and signs the letter)

Go, Sir—you'll add this letter to the courier.

(Secretary bows and leaves.)

(Napoleon to Murat) And now, cousin Murat, and you Davoust my dear Marshall, I am happy to witness, my satisfaction for our entrance to Vilna. The greeting I just received reminded me of that we received in Italy when we were bringing freedom there.

Murat
Polish enthusiasm is admirable. Your Majesty recalls the Colonel of Uhlans at the passage over the Vistula who solicited the authority to swim across the river with his cavaliers before the Emperor's eyes? He lost only about forty men.

Napoleon
I do recall that brave man, I've nominated him for the Legion of Honor.

Davoust
Forty men—that's a figure—Surely, I admire His Majesty, the King of Naples who doesn't fear to expose his soldiers even like himself, but—

Murat
I don't approve of what they say of my soldiers—that my French cavalier has less audacity than the Cossacks.

Napoleon
I don't doubt, that being King Murat you want to show yourself always worthy of that rank. But in a war like this 800 leagues from my capital—one must leave nothing to chance.

Davoust
Our cavalry is already worn out, 8,000 dead horses poison the roads, and Russians are destroying the hay, all the harvest and are preparing a desert in our path: already soldiers are beginning to lack bread.

Napoleon
I am not a man to be frightened by such accidents. Here we are masters—after a few days, of Lithuania—we've cut the Russian

army in two. And the difficulties that oppose us in this place, climate and distance—we were made to conquer—But this campaign which is the decisive campaign of my life will be my last if it is successful. and it will be! Come! It's time I received General Balaschov.

(He signals an aide de camp, who leaves) We will consider later how to give bread to our soldiers.

(Davoust and Murat give a military salute and leave)

Aide de Camp
(Entering, introducing General Balaschov) His Excellency, General Balaschov—aide de camp of His Majesty, the Emperor of Russia.

(He leaves)

Napoleon
(Replying with a nod of the head to the deep bow of Balaschov, and striding straight to him) Hello, General. I've read the letter from the Emperor Alexander that you've brought me and I am very happy to see you. (stares at him) I don't desire, I haven't desired war—but they've forced it on me, I've armed only because they've taken up arms against me, with no thought of attack but with the idea of prudence and just precaution. As I armed I wanted to negotiate, but Russia didn't wish it. Your ambassador, Monsieur Kouraguine, was given the mission of imposing a dishonorable condition on me!—that of retreating to the Vistula and the Oder—and because I didn't wish to accept it for the dignity of my French, your ambassador demanded his passports while refusing passports for mine, Count Lauriston, the honor of being transported to the Emperor Alexander! Complete this attitude with efforts to detach Prussia from its duty—The Entente against me with my worst enemy, England—and judge if it wasn't my right and my duty to place my people on the defense against such provocations. But, even now, such is my desire for conciliation that I am ready to accept all the explanations that you have to give me—

Balaschov
Sire, the Emperor, my Master (Napoleon stares fixedly at Balaschov as if questioning what he can say in reply and Balaschov troubled by this stare, hesitates) Doesn't know....

Napoleon
(Smiling lightly) I am listening, General.

Balaschov
His Majesty, the Emperor Alexander, absolutely faithful to his love for peace and to his great sympathy for your august person, rejects all idea of provocation. He was very astonished to see you violate, without previous declaration, the Russian frontier under pretext of demanding passports made by Kouraguine. The Prince acted without orders and he's been blamed thoroughly. As for the Entente with England, he makes me give his word of honor as a man and a sovereign—that the Government of Russia hasn't contracted any engagement with The London Cabinet.

Napoleon
Not contracted yet.

Balaschov
His Majesty the Emperor Alexander of Russia, being free from all alliances, can still conclude peace on conditions, which since Tilset, have maintained the most perfect understanding between the two Empires. But if his Majesty has no dearer wish than to negotiate with frank cordiality, desiring to be heard.... He doesn't want to open negotiations except on the condition—that no French soldier—that all French troops withdraw behind the Niemen.

Napoleon
(Reacts) I already told you that I desire peace no less than the Emperor Alexander. For the last eighteen months, I did everything to obtain it! Now I've been waiting for an explanation and to begin negotiations they demand that I (Energetic loud gesture)— You demand of me?

Balaschov
The demand of troops, behind the Niemen, Sire.

Napoleon
Behind the Niemen! So now you want me to retreat behind the Niemen!

(He strides toward Balaschov and stares at him) Merely behind the Niemen!

(Balaschov respectfully bows his head) Why you can make such proposals to the Prince of Baden, but not to me! If you gave me Petersburg and Moscow I wouldn't accept such conditions! You say it's I who have declared war! But who then got the first army here? It was the Emperor Alexander, not me. And when I crossed the Niemen it's simply to find myself facing him! It's not my fault if it no longer exists.

Balaschov
But, Sire, my mission proves to Your Majesty….

Napoleon
Your mission! Yes, it's when your situation is bad that you come to propose to treat with me. When after a week of campaigning you recognize that all you can do is retreat when you are cut up, driven from the Polish provinces—when your army revolts.

Balaschov
Sire, permit me to protest—our troops are prepared to die for—

Napoleon
(Interrupting him) My troops are ready to conquer. But I know everything the number and the marching orders of your battalions as well as my own. You have only two hundred thousand men, and I have three times that. As for your allies, the Swedes, the King was mad, they've taken another from my hand—Bernadette, and forgetting where he came from, he's gone mad in his turn, because only a madman can, being Swedish, conclude an alliance with Russia.

Balaschov
But Sire, Sweden, with Russia behind it, is like an inaccessible island.

Napoleon
An isle of fools! And the Turks because you've concluded peace with them, right?

Balaschov
Effectively, Sire, the treaty's been signed.

(An imperceptible gesture of scorn by Napoleon)

Napoleon
Well, they are madmen also—And their cowardice with you shows what their courage against France is worth. And you yourselves, who make a peace which gives you none of the advantages for which you waged war—I allow you to think what you might indeed be! My allies are the Poles—And they will have this reason to conquer—because for them it's death—or the liberation of their fatherland.

Balaschov
Sire—

Napoleon
Your sovereign had a natural ally—France, with the friendship of its Emperor. Ah, what a fine reign Alexander might have had—if he'd wanted it. I would have given him what he was unable to take from the Turks! He would have extended Russia from the Gulf of Bothnia to the mouth of the Danube! He would have been much greater than Catherine the Great! He would have been as I already called him—The Potentate of The North. He would have had the glory of conquering the English, your allies, they too, your allies of tomorrow, and they will be vanquished with you. But he preferred to surround himself with my enemies—with traitors—with subjects revolted from France—and with such blunderers that I prefer to see them with you than with me.

Koutouzov alone is a leader. I saw him at Austerlitz, but he has only one eye. It's true that in a kingdom of the blind—but he's truly too old. Ah, you also have Pful, the ideologue—the man of genius that you sought out aboard to teach you tactics Unfortunately he's not understood by your army. And what role is played by your Emperor in this crowd of nullities?—How does he watch them doing nothing? They compromise him—they make all their faults weigh on him. And why has the Emperor Alexander taken command of the troops? Why's that? War is my affair—his job is to reign and not to command troops. A sovereign must only be in an army of which he is general. But you know what he's gained by coming to provoke me? I'm going push you back beyond the Dvina and the Dnieper—and I'm going to distribute to my own allies, the prerogatives that I had destined for him; I will revive that barrier that Europe was blind enough, and criminal enough, to allow to fall, I will drive the Empire of the Tsar's into the deserts and Steppes of Siberia

(Napoleon takes a few agitated steps then stops facing Balaschov) Still, what a beautiful reign your Master might have had.

Balaschov
May Your Majesty excuse me, But I shall dare to tell him that while recognizing the valor of the French army, and the genius of the one who commands it—we do not yet despair in Russia of the result of the struggle in which we are engaged. We will fight with determination with despair, even, and God will doubtless favor a war which we believe more just as we sought it less.

Napoleon
Sought it less! But I don't hold your sovereign entirely responsible. I know quite well that the mischief makers who surround him have brought about the misunderstanding between our two countries, yes, without them it's in friendship and alliance that I'd be visiting his Empire—curious country, yours, general: Moscow, your capital is a very interesting city. How many inhabitants...?

Balaschov
Around three hundred thousand, Sire.

Napoleon
Moscow's called, Holy Moscow, right?

Balaschov
Yes, Sire.

Napoleon
Many churches? How many?

Balaschov
Two hundred, Sire.

Napoleon
Two hundred! Why so many churches?

Balaschov
The Russians are very pious.

Napoleon
Yes, in Poland and especially in Russia—convents multiply And the huge number of churches and monasteries is a sad symptom of the condition of a country—it denotes a singular retardation in civilization.

Balaschov
Sire, each country has its mores and its institutions and what doesn't suit one may suit another.

Napoleon
No, no! It doesn't depend on location but on the times. Convents no longer suit the present century, and, except among you—one doesn't find more in Europe.

Balaschov
I beg pardon to Your Majesty, but there are many convents and churches not only in Russia, but also in Spain.

Napoleon
Yes, that's a country of fanaticism. But let's get back to Moscow—what's the most direct route?

Balaschov
Sire, as all roads led to Rome, all roads lead to Moscow!—The most notable one, which was chosen by Charles XII—The road though Poltava.

Napoleon
General, I don't yet know the way to defeat. The one I've taken has led me straight here. It's actually here in the working office of the Emperor Alexander? Yes, it was here ten days ago that he discussed again with my personal enemies, measures to be taken to stop my march. And now I am here in the place he occupied—you say nothing, admirer and courtier of the Emperor Alexander?

(Goes to Balaschov and tugs him gently by the ear) But despite the provocations that he employed against me, I haven't lost my personal esteem for him. And you will convey my regrets that my duty forbids me to give in to my sympathy? (Stamps his foot twice. Two chamberlains enter bearing the Emperor's hat, gloves, and kerchief. Napoleon takes these different objects) You are dining with us, General.

Balaschov
I thank Your Majesty.

Napoleon
You will deliver my letter to the Emperor Alexander—

(To his chamberlain) Give the order to prepare my best horses for the General. He's got a long way to go.

CURTAIN

ACT III

Scene 4

The Rostov's home in Moscow. A huge lordly mansion—a verandah giving on a great wooded garden. One notices an enormous oak spreading its branches. At rise, Natasha is singing accompanying herself at the harpsichord. Douniacha—seated in an armchair near the window, knits quietly.

Natasha
O mio crudele affetto oh—mio– (Stopping) Ah—how unhappy I am—

(She goes mechanically to look at the verandah)

Douniacha
Don't be impatient, my little pigeon—he will come back—

Natasha
No, my old Douniacha, never!

(She returns to the piano and resumes) Oh, mio crudele.

(Stopping anew) Still, this Natasha's a charmer! She has everything going for her—a ravishing face!

(She looks at herself in a mirror) She's very intelligent—And what a voice!

(She plays a roulade) Oh, it's not to say a superb voice!

(She repeats a roulade and returns to the piano) Oh mio crudele affeto O mio crudele Oh mio. No, no! I can't do it anymore, I cannot do it— (She slams the instrument closed impatiently)

Sonia (entering)
What fury! What have you done to our harpsichord?

Natasha
Oh! My Sonia, my little cousin—How glad I am to see you.

Sonia
And what about me, my darling? But we saw each other just now.

Natasha
Oh—I'd like to see you all the time. Because we are such friends, such friends. Friends for life. (Pulling up her sleeve and pointing to a little mark on her arm) You know this little scar. The burn mark I made with steel in sign of friendship with you.

Sonia
Dear mad woman (Hugs her)

Natasha
It's so nice to have an alter ego to whom you can talk.

Sonia
Do you have something to hide?

Natasha
Oh—I don't wish to be made fun of! I don't want anyone to pity me! My situation is so painful, so ridiculous even. A young girl abandoned.

Sonia
Don't torture yourself. He'll come back.

Douniacha
There you see plainly, my little soul—just what I told you.

Natasha
Ah, leave me alone, now—now! No, he'll never come back.

(Douniacha leaves)

No, no, I feel it! Never! It's over. I had made such a dream of it. Three weeks he hasn't seen me. But tell me what he said to me! To cradle me with words—And then suddenly, to disappear! What have I done to him? Yet, he seemed—to love me!

Sonia
And you, did you love him?

Natasha
I don't know. But the first time that I saw him I felt an unusual unease—

Sonia
Remember, others have already paid court to you . And they seemed to please you—! Boris, Dennisov.

Natasha
No, I've never felt anything like it. I was ill at ease with him. I was scared! Was that love?

Sonia
How would I know?

Natasha
You—you know will enough if Nicholas scares you.

Sonia
Natasha, you say that you love me and you torture me! Why speak of the impossible? What would your mother say, our mother? She'd say that I have no heart; that I am rewarding her for all her kindness by ruining the career of her son! No, no, I swear it. (Crossing herself) I love you all too much. I am too grateful not to sacrifice myself. Oh, yes, yes—to sacrifice all to you. But I have nothing.

Natasha
And you call me crazy, Sonia! It's you who are crazy to think this way! Sacrifice yourself! Why it's Nicholas's happiness you are sacrificing. He adores you. Remember how jealous he was when Dolokhov was hovering around you! But I want my little cousin to be happy! It's not a reason that because I, myself am very unhappy, that—

Sonia
No, no, you don't deserve to be and you won't be.

Natasha
(Getting hold of herself) Well, no, I won't be. I no longer want to think about it! He came, well, he won't come anymore. We lived well enough before we knew him! First of all, it's true he scared me. It's better that it be thus, I will not marry! That's all! Never! Never! I will stay here where I'm loved and I will live very calmly! What is it I want? To be left in peace! Let me be left in peace!

(She bursts into tears)

Sonia
(Enfolding her in her arms) My poor darling! My poor darling!

(They embrace and cling to each other)

Douniacha
(Running in) Natasha! Natasha! Do you know who's come?

Natasha and Sonia
(Together) Who is it?

Douniacha
Our dear little master, Nicholas. He' is getting off his horse in the courtyard.

Natasha
(A bit down) Ah, Nicholas! (Getting control) What joy! Well you are satisfied.

Sonia
Oh, yes! But I don't want to see him now. (She wants to flee but Natasha holds her hand)

Natasha
Stay put!

(Nicholas enters seemingly preoccupied. Douniacha kisses his hand and leaves)

Natasha
Nikolenka! What a surprise! (They embrace) How were you able to leave your Regiment?

Nicholas
A mission to our father the Marshall of the Nobility. Is he here?

Natasha
He's going to be back. He left about some sale of I don't know what. (Nicholas reacts) But Mama is here?

Nicholas
Yes—I saw her. I kissed her.

Natasha
Well, Sonia is here, too. Sonia wanted to run away—and yet you will still be happy to see her.

Nicholas
My sweet Sonia. She doesn't want to hug me?

Sonia
Oh, yes, dear Nicholas.

(They hug)

Nicholas
But why'd you want to flee?

Natasha
Because she loves, you.

Sonia
Natasha—mercy.

Natasha
You remember what you said to each other before your departure—She wants you to forget everything! She's very noble—it's very handsome—but it's very crazy and nasty too, because I want my only friend to become my sister.

Nicholas
I never take back my word.

Natasha
(Interrupting him) No, not that. I knew quite well you would say that. But it's not necessary. It's not from respect for your pledged word that you ought to marry her, but from love.

Sonia
No—I don't have the right, I am poor.

Natasha
Perhaps there's something beside money in the world!

Nicholas
Ah, money! Why, yes—we will be happy without it—(Kissing Sonia's hand) Sonia will be my wife.

Natasha
Come on! There will be, at least, happiness in the house. Ah, here's Papa.

Nicholas
Leave us, my darlings.

Natasha
So be it! Let's respect secrets of state.

(The girls leave)

Count Rostov
(Entering and very preoccupied) You here, my son! Not wounded, not ill?

Nicholas
No, Papa, I'm fine. My regiment has not yet joined the army—and I've obtained leave to come to you here.

Count Rostov
And what have you come to announce to me? Nothing bad I hope? (Lighting a big pipe) because I am indeed worn out. I struggle in difficulties. Vera's dowry, the Countess is always in need of money—it's a heavy expense. She's an extravagant spender.. The war has killed all credit. I've re-mortgaged everything and now it's necessary to sell, and these days it's hard to find a buyer. Do you know what they offered me for the property in Tambov? Fifty thousand roubles. It's worth two hundred thousand! Anyway, what have you come to tell me?

Nicholas
(Assuming a casual air with difficulty) Papa—I can see I've picked a bad time—it's because I too, I need money.

Count Rostov
Ah, you can say you picked a bad time. But, scamp, a month ago I delivered 2,000 roubles to you, and you gave me your word of honor—though I didn't ask for it—to be more economical, satanic child! Still, one must hold one's rank. Still, we'll find it, you don't need much—

Nicholas
Much—I lost a little—That is to say—yes, a lot.

Count Rostov
Well, tell me how much?

Nicholas
43,000 roubles.

Count Rostov
(Stupefied, exclaiming) What! Lost with whom? You're joking.

Nicholas
With Dolokhov.

Count Rostov
Dolokhov—Why, he was degraded after his duel. How were you able to gamble with him? You, an officer.

Nicholas
It took place in a club of friends—It was an impulse. I wanted to win a hundred roubles so as to offer it to Mama for her birthday, to give her that little box she talks about so much—and I lost, lost. That Dolokhov is terrible. He refused my note and I promised to pay him tomorrow.

Count Rostov
(Letting his pipe fall. In a dull voice) Well—!

Nicholas
(In a careless tone) What to do? Who doesn't have things like this happen?

Count Rostov
Yes, yes it's difficult,—it's going to be difficult to find it—To, whom doesn't this happen? Yes—to whom doesn't this happen?

(He looks furtively at his son's face and starts to leave)

Nicholas
(Seizing his hand and kissing it) Father—little father! Forgive me! How good you are. And I who dared to speak to you in this tone. I ought to beg your pardon on my knees. I'm a coward!

Count Rostov
No, no! You are a good lad! All the same it's worth more than a cannonball. One doesn't die of it. I will leave him—the domain of Tambov. But your Dolokhov will be paid. The important thing is that my Nikolenka—my handsome squadron leader do honor to our name and to his rank! Hug me—but, I'll need to give you enough money for the little box.

Nicholas
(Falling in his arms) Papa.

Count Rostov
(Berg Enters) Ah, a nice surprise for you, your comrade Nicholas!

(Nicholas and Berg shake hands)

Berg
(To Nicholas) I'm enchanted to see you. For goodness sakes—you won't see Vera—she remained in our installation in Petersburg—oh—one must never leave a house unwatched. Especially such a new house. Ah, we have a pretty installation, all new furniture, and on that subject

(To Count) Vera told me to ask you if we might have the little round Chinese table in the large salon?

Count Rostov
Ah—that's the Countess' affair!

Berg
Our house warming party was a true success, very considerable people came! As for me, I had to come here for business matters and actually have, my dear father-in-law, some very vexing things to tell you. I've just come back from Skwortzov—he refuses to discount your note, the note of 80,000 roubles—which you so paternally subscribed to.

Count Rostov
He refuses! Ah—That's the last straw!

Nicholas
My poor Papa!

Berg
Ah, yes, poor Papa, we are really to be pitied! But they told me that your situation was embarrassed—that the war imposes new expenses on you—that even your title of Marshal of the Nobility entails great expenses!

Count Rostov
Yes! Yes! But don't worry my lad, you will be paid on the due date.

Berg
Oh—I know it quite well, my father—But people are so suspicious—

Count Rostov
You can reassure them. First of all I am renouncing my function of Marshall of the Nobility!

Berg
Oh!

Count Rostov
I'm forced to do so. And then I'm selling the domain of Tambov.

Berg
Ah—my dear father, don't do anything precipitously. Your title of Marshall of the Nobility gives to our family an importance that it would be vexing to be deprived of. And the estate—are you selling it on good terms?

Count Rostov
Barely a quarter of its worth.

Berg
Ah—in that case you must wait. It will be a great burden for us—but we must sacrifice for the interests of the family.

Count Rostov
No, no—some debts won't wait (Looks at Nicholas).

Nicholas
Father, pardon, pardon—

Berg
But I will wait, I will wait. Ah, but an idea—How much are you selling Tambov for?

Count Rostov
A miselry—50,000 roubles.

Berg
Impossible! Why everything can be arranged! Give me the domain in payment for your note.

Count Rostov
You are really sweet, my lad, but I need money right away. (Rings, servant enters) Let someone go find Skwortzov. (Servant leaves)

Berg
Oh, look, Nicholas, join with me; it's absolutely necessary to prevent your father from taking desperate resolutions.

A servant
His Excellency, Count Pierre Kirilovitch Bezhoukov.

Count Rostov
Pierre Bezhoukov? Quick show him in! I'm in haste to embrace him! (Going to Pierre and hugging him. The servant leaves) My dear friend.

Pierre
Excuse me!—but barely returned to my empty house in Moscow, I needed to warm up again in the heart of a friendly family! And I came to find you. Here I hope, at least, that everyone is happy. But you are not alone.

Count Rostov
Oh—I'm with my son Nicholas and my son-in-law.

Pierre
(Shaking Nicholas' hand) How are you? (To Berg) Enchanted to see you, Captain Berg.

Berg
No, Count, Commander Berg!

Pierre
Compliments! Vera—pardon, Madame Berg—is in good health?

Berg
Perfect—we are now installed in Peters—

Count Rostov
(cutting him off) How glad I am to see you, and to see you living well! I heard of the result of your duel! Ah—I was in great fear for you.

Pierre
Oh—perhaps it would have been better if I'd remained. What a horrible and absurd thing. It haunts me. I still have the vision of

Dolokhov falling in the snow which he reddened with his blood! I wanted to cross the limits, to run towards him. I heard someone say: If you please—keep your place! Then he got up, fired, missed me and fell back face down on the ground. Stupid! And the lie of all that! Why? Why? Attitudes! Nothing real about it. Mortal gestures without hate! Ah, when I thought I would have killed him!

Count Rostov
So, no one is dead!

Pierre
And it's only ridiculous!

Berg
Yes. But he was degraded! That's a hard punishment—to have worked to obtain a fine grade, a beautiful position! Then to find oneself nothing at all! A soldier who fights like a serf laborer.

Nicholas
Ah! Dolokhov will yet get himself noticed. He's determined to do everything.

Pierre
He's a man of war. A man of prey! His sort have a lot to do, because the work of hate has begun.

Count Rostov
The work of hate! But also the work of love for the fatherland.

Berg
It's begun to be dangerous, to speak French in the streets; it's to the point where Prince Galitzine has taken a Russian tutor. He's learning Russian.

Count Rostov
The Emperor has just arrived in Moscow.

Berg
That will perhaps be the opportunity to get His Majesty to agree to my services in the Guard.

Pierre
I thought he had decided to remain with the army.

Count Rostov
No, but he wanted to inspire the troops by his presence.

Nicholas
He succeeded! What love! What enthusiasm!

Berg
On campaign one doesn't know what it is to fall in love. Accordingly,—they are smitten with the Emperor.

Nicholas
Oh, no joking on that subject! A feeling so great, so noble!

Berg
Oh—I was only repeating a saying in the camp—Because I too share in it—I approve.

Nicholas
No, no! You don't understand. You cannot understand! Oh—the joy of dying! Not to save the life of the Emperor, that would be too fine!—but simply to die before his eyes.

Berg
Oh—Rather be gloriously wounded and noticed by him!

Count Rostov
And now, our father, after visiting the soldiers is coming to visit his people in the capital. Everywhere he intends to spread the spirit of the national war. For tomorrow, he's convoked the nobility and merchants in the Slobotzki Palace. You'll be there, Count Bezhoukov?

Pierre
(With great emotion) His Majesty wants to consult us by joining the different orders, nobles and merchants—this will be then a sort of Estates-General—according to the principles of the French Revolution—of the social contract.

Nicholas
Oh—Count, The French Revolution has nothing do with this—dreams we must abandon if we are the sons of Russia.

Pierre
Why, I suppose that the nobility, besides expressing its enthusiasm and its sympathy, is being called also to judge the means by which we must aid the country. I think that The Emperor himself would be dissatisfied if he found in us only proprietors who will give him their peasants to make cannon fodder—and if he get no advice from us.

Count Rostov
No, my dear Pierre, we have only to answer the call of the Emperor and to give him whatever he asks for. His trip will triple the strength of the army, and if our Master really intends to appoint the leader according to our heart.

Berg
Why what leader would be better than our great tactician Barclay?

Count Rostov
He who possesses something better than all the tactics: a Russian soul—Our old Koutouzov. It's a Russian who will save Russia.

Berg
But can they name as Generalissimo a man who cannot mount a horse, almost blind—who sleeps in Council meetings, a man, in the end, (lowering his voice) of depraved morals?

Count Rostov
My word; he acquired them among the Turks who he beat so well, that we can pardon him. And believe indeed, commander that's even without his horse he'll always be up front, and as for his seeing with only one eye, he sees more clearly with it than most who have two.

Berg
Oh—what I was saying about him, is only through hearsay—I would not allow myself an opinion of a general who might become our serenissimo. Unfortunately, His Majesty doesn't like him.

Count Rostov
Our father loves his country above all. Your great German tacticians have shown what they know how to do—pull back—always back.

Nicholas
And the enemy is already in Vitebsk, four marches from Smolensk

Count Rostov
Now it's a question of defending the very heart of Russia. Did you think, Pierre Kirilovitch, that when they mobilized the Militia it would be necessary for you to mount a horse?

Pierre
Yes, yes—in warfare. But as for me, what sort of soldier am I? Yes it's all so strange! So strange! At present no one can be sure of anything! But I am so far from military tastes.

Nicholas
(Getting heated) Oh, Count! There's nothing happier! It's plain you don't know a soldier's life. Ah, if you knew what one experiences, when after a leave, when one returns to one's corps! The sight of the first Hussar that I meet sauntering before the casern rejoices my heart! And the comrades who make a celebration over you. Brothers—in-arms, who embrace you! I experience the same feeling returning to my regiment as I do in returning to the house of my father. Because the regiment is also a home, a home agreeable and dear, like that of our parents.

Pierre
But you are no longer a free man—you must submit to an exacting discipline.

Nicholas
Why, that's one charm the more. That's what completes the resemblance to home. You experience the same calm, the same comfort—and the same consciousness of being in one's place. Here, in the regiment, all is simple and clear. The world is divided into two unequal sections. One: our regiment from Pavlograd—the other, everybody else. And the others don't count! In the regiment, everything is known—who's the lieutenant, who's the captain—who's good, who's bad—and in particular—who's a good comrade and who's a bad one—The sutler gives credit—every four months you receive your wages; there's nothing to invent or to choose—one only abstains from what is judged bad in the Pavlograd regiment. One must do what is plain and clearly required —and everything is fine.

Pierre
Yes, I conceive the charm of this fraternal life. But why must this love change into murder?

Nicholas
Don't call a soldier's duty "murder".

Pierre
(Aside) Duty.

Countess Rostov
(Enters very preoccupied to Count) Ely! (seeing Bezhoukov) Hello, Piotr Kirilovitch.

Count Rostov
What's wrong, my pigeon?

Countess Rostov
I'm in mortal unease.

Nicholas
What's wrong, Mama?

Countess Rostov
Because of Peter (to Bezhoukov), your godson. Ivan saw him leave by the small gate. He'd put on his finest clothes.

Berg
Maternal unease—He must have gone to his comrades; it's not the first time.

Countess Rostov
But this morning we had a scene with him.

Nicholas
A scene?

Count Rostov
Yes, this morning he renewed his demand to be allowed to enlist.

Pierre
You refused him again?

Count Rostov
I sent him to school.

Countess Rostov
If you had seen that poor child! he was so desperate, so pale, so pale. Hopefully he hasn't committed some folly. As if it wasn't enough with my Nicholas! Must they again take my baby from me!

Natasha
(Entering with Sonia) Mama! Mama!

Sonia
Mother! Don't be frightened!

Countess Rostov
What? What's the matter? Petia?

Natasha
Yes, they're bringing him here.

Countess Rostov
Bringing him here? Is he injured…?

Natasha
No, no—nothing's wrong with him

(Enter Petia, half fainted supported by a soldier, a merchant woman, and servants)

Merchant woman
There, there, gently.

Countess Rostov
(Rushing to Pierre whom she covers with kisses) My Petia, my sweetheart. Speak, speak to me.

Petia
Ah Mama, I saw him! (He falls exhausted into an armchair—they all go to him)

Count Rostov
But what's happened?

Soldier
Be without fear, Excellency. I was able to protect the little lord. I noticed him in the crowd which was waiting in front of the Kremlin to acclaims our father, the Tsar—

Merchant Lady
And there was a lot of shoving! They pushed and they pushed. My beautiful silk shawl was all torn up—But he was pushed harder than the others. He shouted—"Let me pass! I have a petition to deliver to him!" It's a miracle he wasn't suffocated. Poor cherub, it was a shame!

Soldier
He's a brave little lord! If you had seen him when His Majesty tossed gifts to the people—He'd have let himself be crushed to get one! That's easy to understand. A cake touched by the Emperor.

Petia
(Coming to) The Emperor! I saw him! How handsome he is! How noble! An angel—Hurrah! Yes, I was able to shout my Hurrah!

Countess Rostov
Calm down my son! (To Soldier and Merchant Lady) Thanks my good friends! We'll take care of you.

(To Sonia) Darling, I commend these brave folks to you

Sonia
Fine, Mama.

(Sonia leads the Soldier and Merchant Lady off)

Natasha
Oh, how I would have liked to be with you, dear Petia.

(She hugs him)

Petia
(Noticing Nicholas) Nicholas! What luck!

Count Rostov
My son, you gave us quite a turn.

Petia
Ah, Papa! I couldn't hold back any longer! Since you refused me, I wanted to go find Our Father, to beg him to send me against the enemy.

(Reaction by the Countess)

Count Rostov
Petia, will you shut up! Look at the trouble you are causing your mother! Before going to fight, finish your studies.

Petia
No, I can no longer learn anything now that the country is in danger. My classmate Fedia Obolensky has already gone. He's younger than I am. I'm really sad to cause mother pain. But if you won't let me leave, well, I will run away! Nothing, nothing in the world will prevent me from doing my duty.

Pierre
(Who's followed this with conflicting emotions) Duty! Duty! Yes, Count Rostov—since Petia insists on going, allow him to serve in my regiment!

Petia
Ah, my dear Godfather, thanks—

Count Rostov
Your regiment?

Pierre
Yes, I've understood at last! And tomorrow I will announce to His Majesty that I am placing a thousand men, and myself at his disposition.

Count Rostov
That's fine, Pierre (shaking both his hands) Yes, everything for the country. Come on, Petia—hug your mother—we are going to sign your enlistment—

Countess Rostov
My poor child!

Petia
Don't cry, Mama—never has your Petia been as happy as he is today.

Countess Rostov
My darling! Why you are in tatters! Come with me, let Mama dress you once again as when you were little.

(She leaves with Petia)

Berg
Ah! Heavens! In my emotion, I forgot to ask her about the table.

(He rushes to follow her)

A Servant
Excellency, Monsieur Skwortzov has just arrived!

Count Rostov
Fine (To Pierre) I'm going to ask you for a moment—I have to settle some business that admits of no delay. Come, Nicholas.

Pierre
Why, I'm going to take my leave—

Natasha
Oh—Count—don't leave like that. I would like to ask you something.

Count Rostov
I'll leave you both. Till soon....

(He leaves with Nicholas)

Pierre
And what have you to tell me, dear little Natasha?

Natasha
Oh, nothing important. It was rather the pleasure of chatting with a friend.

Pierre
Oh! Yes, a friend!

Natasha
By the way, friend, what's become of your inseparable—Prince André?

Pierre
Your fiancé?

Natasha
My fiancé? But he's never been my fiancé. And in any case, he no longer is!

Pierre
(With an instinctive reaction of joy) Is it possible? What's happened?

Natasha
Why nothing at all! One fine day he ceased to give news of himself. Doubtless he must have found. Natasha Rostov no longer worth his trouble to pay court to!

Pierre
Oh—don't believe that! It's impossible that once touched by your charm he would be capable of forgetting you— What! he would have had the joy of being able to join his life to the best and most charming creature— No, no! It's because he's been

detained, prevented for some time by something we don't know about. But myself even, I am without news of him for several weeks. His service, a mission, what do I know? Don't torture yourself, dear Natasha!

Natasha
Oh, trust me I'm not torturing myself. You presented the Prince to me: coming on the part of my great friend Pierre, he seemed nice to me. But truly you mustn't believe that I regret, that I—

(At this moment André appears on the veranda, Natasha screams joyfully) There he is!

(Kissing Pierre) Ah, my friend!

(She runs away. Pierre follows Natasha with a mournful look)

André
Pierre! (Entering) What joy to find you in this house!

Pierre
They are waiting for you with impatience.

André
And as for me, I hesitated to return

Pierre
When happiness awaits you?

André
That's precisely the question. I've thought it over a lot.

Pierre
Is that why you've been so slow to return?

André
It's because I went to see my father—to ask for his consent—

Pierre
And he gave it to you?

André
Yes—but not willingly—and by imposing as a condition that the marriage not take place for a year. He said so many things to me.

Evidently, this marriage displeases him with respect to the relations, to the fortune, to nobility. But that's nothing for me. The

Rostov's are fine and good people. But my father made me observe that I am already no longer young and that Natasha is still only a child—and his irony froze me. I remembered that life had already displayed to me disenchantments.

Pierre
No one has had a life crueler than mine. And yet I feel happiness exists. All men, you see, have their role prepared for them, but many still never possess it. Some because they let it escape, others because they renounce it for a more worthy cause— But first of all—you love her?

André
Ah, my friend, yes I love her! I would never believed anyone would have said of me that I could love so much—I love almost to the point of being ill of it; but I wouldn't give up this illness for anything in the world. Above all, I wasn't living. It's only now that I'm living where she is—happiness and hope—where she is not— sadness, darkness—

Pierre
Yes, yes—darkness, shadows. I understand—

André
But she, can she love me? Can she?—Why don't you say something—

Pierre
Me? Me? What have I to say? (Controlling himself) Well, André, since you love her—learn this: she loves you.

André
Don't talk craziness!

Pierre
She loves you. I know it! If you'd seen her anxiety, her sorrow, while waiting for you—and the explosion of joy when you appeared. She loves you and you will be happy.

André
Ah, my friend, my friend! Must the joy of my life come from you? No, I cannot renounce my happiness. I cannot not love light. Ah, now I understand the lesson the old tree gave me when I entered the house of my beloved. At my last visit the old oak was all black and dry. But just now, I no longer recognized it—it was like an immense tent of verdure—shaking under the gold of a setting sun—one could not see its twisted limbs nor its wounds,

nor its defiant age and sorrow: on the hard centenarian back young leaves were shining, unfolding joyously toward life! It was a renewal, it was renewal, it was the future.

Pierre
Yes, the future, the radiant future. And me, too, I am quite happy.

(Enter the Countess followed by Natasha)

Countess Rostov
(To André) It's been a long while we've had the future.

André
(Kissing the hand of the Countess, and bows to Natasha) I didn't come to you all this time, because I was at my father's. I had to speak to him about something very important.

Pierre
Countess, I am taking leave of you.

Countess Rostov
Till soon, my dear Count.

André
To you also, Countess, I have something very important to say.

Countess Rostov
(To Natasha, who remains motionless looking at André) Go, Natasha—escort our friend Bezhoukov—come back soon—

Natasha
(Aside, leaving) Like this, right away! immediately—No, it's impossible.

(She crosses herself and looks at the icon. She leaves with Pierre)

Countess Rostov
I am all yours, Prince!

André
Countess, I've come to ask you for the hand of your daughter.

Countess Rostov
(After a short silence, and with some annoyance) Your proposition—is agreeable to us. I accept it, and I'm happy over it. But this depends on herself.

André
I will ask her thoughts when I've got your consent. You are giving it to me?

Countess Rostov
Yes. (She kisses André's face; he kisses her hand) I will be happy to have you for a son—my husband will consent, I'm persuaded of that. But your father….

André
My father places on his consent an absolute condition—that however long the war lasts—The marriage will not take place in less than a year.

Countess Rostov
So be it! We will respect his wishes. Besides, Natasha is still very young. Here she is, coming back. I am leaving you with her.

Natasha
(Entering, all a-tremble) Mama!

Countess Rostov
Prince André Bolkonski is asking us for your hand.

(She kisses Natasha and leaves)

André
I've loved you since I saw you—Can I hope?

(Natasha goes to him, he kisses her hand) Do you love me?

Natasha
(Sighing) Yes, yes—(She weeps)

André
Why cry? What's wrong with you?

Natasha
Ah, I am so happy! (Smiling between her tears)

André
(Holding her hands) You've got to know Natasha, that our marriage cannot be celebrated for a year—

Natasha
(Without thinking) Fine! Fine!

André
Forgive me. You are so young and I've lived so much already. Surely, I am aware of a duty at the same time so sweet and grave that binds me too you forever. But I'm afraid for you who don't know me—This year's delay which is so painful for me.—will allow you to examine yourself and to consider. In a year I will ask you to make my happiness. But you are free. Our engagement will remain secret, and if you perceive that you no longer love me—or if you still love me—

Natasha
Why do you say this? You know that since the day you came to Otradnoie, I loved you.

André
In a year you might—

Natasha
(Finally understanding) A year! Why, a year? Why?

André
It's my father's will.

Natasha
Is not possible otherwise?

André
Besides, the war is on, which forcibly postpones all plans.

Natasha
This is terrible! No! It's frightful. I will die of this delay. It's impossible! It's frightful!

André
It's forced! Now I have something to ask of you. I'm going to leave. God knows what can happen. You've known Bezhoukov for a long while. He's your friend.

Natasha
Yes, he's nice, but is very comical—

André
He's the best of friends and my best friend. Well—if something happens while I'm not here....

Natasha
What can happen?

André
Some misfortune may take place—I ask you to address yourself to him, to him alone for advice and help. By confiding in him—it will be as if you are confiding in me myself.

Natasha
Yes—but it won't be you.

André
Natasha, is it really true that you love me?

Natasha
(Offering him her hand) I am happy—

(André takes her hand and pulls her into his arms)

CURTAIN

ACT III

Scene 5

After Smolensk

A Russian camp on the route to Moscow. A cantina near the audience on the right. Further back on the left, a Headquarters. Before the curtain rises, military noises: drums, trumpets, singing, etc.

At rise, soldiers can be seen grouped in picturesque poses. Lieutenant Touchine is seated at the Cantina removing his boots.

Petrov
(Coming in with his comrades) Let's go! Yet another review—Ah, my friends. What mud!

Touchine
(Removing his boots and calling the sutler) Hey, Bikov! Take these. Take these from me—(Giving him boots) Let them dry before your fire!

Petrov
Ah, if I dared I would do much more! That's always been my dream. To make war with warm feet. I had a stolen pair of slippers from the French! But they were stolen from me. Of real imitation leather. Now that's an army of thieves.

Makeev
There's something in all this—these are brave, noble! It's an astonishing people.

Zikine
But they are more astonishing when they are dead, they're tidy, neat and white like birch trees—Peasants who gathered up the cadavers at Smolensk told me—tidy like white paper, not rotten at all—whereas ours—

Petrov
It comes from diet, for sure they must steal chefs the usual way.

Tikhone
Well, since they are white when they die we are going to send them all to the laundry.

Zikine
If they'd only give us Koutouzov for a leader, their Emperor would be captured.

Makeev
Ah, for that, no way! If one thinks one's got him, he changes into a bird, an eagle and flies off! That's the real truth.

Petrov
Possibly! But as for me, if I ever catch him I will pierce him with an aspen stake, and I'll bring him alive. Then will see if he flies off.

Makeev
That would be great! He's made so many die.

(Enter an NCO)

NCO
What are you screwing, around here for? The commander's coming with the General. I've just caught it because of you. The review was a shame! Ah, drunks! I will make you see indeed. (He hits Makeev) You couldn't make a bit less noise.

Makeev
(Aside) He could hit a bit less hard. I think he broke my jaw.

(The General and the Commandant enter)

General
Ah, this is pretty! Flattering to look at. Soon you'll put your men in dressing gowns! But I will teach you how soldiers must be dressed for the review! My Goodness, here's one in socks. Why he's an officer! Lieutenant Touchine you have no shame in your

capacity you must give a correct example and you are there, without boots. If the alarm were sounded you'd be very well without boots to run against the enemy.

Touchine
General—The men say they are more agile without boots.

General
Then it's your men who are making you march! Go get your boots on, sir, and respect your rank more. (Touchine salutes and leaves) By the way—who is this soldier I saw in your battalion dressed like a Hungarian?

Commander
Your Excellency—

General
Eh, what? Your Excellency? Your Excellency? And what's wrong Your Excellency? Do you know him, yes or no?

Commander
Your Excellency—it's Dolokhov—the degraded!

General
Well—send to find this Dolokhov for me—this degraded. (The commander gestures to a Sergeant Major who leaves) But degraded in what way? As field Marshall or as soldier? If he's no more than a simple soldier he must be dressed as a simple soldier—that's the rule.

Commander
Your Excellency, you yourself authorized him to dress like this on marches.

General
Authorized! Authorized! It's always like this with the old generation. They tell you something and you understand. Authorized! I never authorized him to dress in— (Enter Dolokhov) Ah, there he is! Incredible! Come on—straighten up, if you please. What have you got? Where's your foot? Your foot, where is it? (Dolokhov pulls back his foot while looking boldly at the General) Why do you have a blue cloak? Do you want me to take it off you? Sergeant! You'll dress him for me according to the rules! I will screw you—with blue coats!—Rascal—

Dolokhov
General, my duty is to obey your orders—but I am not obliged to endure—

General
No speaking in the ranks. No speaking. Not a word! Not a word!

Dolokhov
(In a deep voice) I am not obliged to endure insults.

(Reaction by the General that Dolokhov stops by looking at him fixedly)

General
(Pulling his scarf, nervously) Please change your clothes immediately!

(Dolokhov salutes, pivots and follows the Sergeant Major)

General
And the rest of you, a little care for your uniform if you please! Before your officers you might assume a military posture, bunch of swine!

(Leaves with the Sergeant Major)

Bikov
That wasn't good in front of the Sergeant-Major. The road's not safe. Too many officers.

Zikine
You are right. The Pope said—"You will avoid bad company."

(They leave)

Dennisov
(Counting money in a purse) Heavens, old friend, we are rich! And you see it's government money, nothing but new coins—Would you do me the service of locking this under our tent?

Nicholas
Very gladly—but here's your man—I'm leaving you.

Dennisov
You don't like Lieutenant Telianine?

Nicholas
Why, no one in the regiment does!

Dennisov
Not even me! Still, he's correct—

Nicholas
I don't say otherwise but I have a sort of instinctive repulsion for him—Besides he was sent from The Guard.

Dennisov
Yes—no one ever learned why—

Telianine
Greetings, gentlemen.

Nicholas
(Coldly) Hello, Lieutenant, hello (Shaking his hand with some hesitation, to Dennisov) Where do we need to put the money?

Dennisov
Hide it under the pillow—Lavrouchka is such a slob—

Nicholas
Understood.

(He leaves)

Telianine
Well, Captain! How do you like your horse—my Gratchik?

Dennisov
He's a fine animal—I paid a good price for him—

Telianine
You got a good deal.

Dennisov
Still he's beginning to limp with his left hind foot a bit.

Telianine
It's the shoe that's broken. It's nothing—I will show you which nail needs to be fixed—It's not a secret!

Dennisov
Well go see to it immediately and you will explain to me.

Telianine
At your orders, Captain. And you will thank me for the excellent opportunity

(Heading off. Enter Marshal of lodging)

Marshal
Captain the Colonel is asking for you.

Dennisov
Screwed up profession. Not a moment to oneself. Lieutenant would you wait for me in my tent—fourth on the left, second avenue.

Telianine
With pleasure, Captain.

(Dennisov heads out with the NCO, Telianine heads for Dennisov's tent)

(A small carriage drawn by a donkey led in hand by a soldier—followed by the Commander who rushes to stop it)

Commander
(To Soldier) Stop! Stop! Who allowed you to pass this way, scum? Come on—turn around and be quick about it—

Soldier
But Commander—

Commander
Ah, you reply—Just you wait (Raises his whip, but the Soldier avoids the blow which falls on the donkey's blanket)

Woman
(In the carriage, leaping out) Help! Help!

(Seeing André emerging from the Headquarters tent) Officer! Help—in the name of God, protect us. I am the wife of the doctor of the Seventh Scouts. We've lost the regiment. We must get to it.

Commander
You must get out of here.

(To Soldier) Be gone!—Or I'll beat you into a pudding! Get back with your slut.

Woman
Monsieur Aide de Camp, protect us!

André
(To Commandant) Sir! You see plainly she's a woman. Let this carriage pass.

Commander
Did you hear! Stop! Brute!

André
Let her pass, I tell you.

Commander
(To André) And you—who are you? Are you the chief here? I'm in command here

(To Soldier) Do you hear! Get going! Get back! Or I'll beat you to a pulp.

André
Would you let her pass—?

Commandant
(To André) Ah—you!

André
(Raising his baton) Let them pass.

Commander
(Furious) (To Soldier) Go ahead, pass (Aside) These officers of The Headquarters! Working with them is impossible!

Prince André
What leaders! Cads—and not Soldiers.

Dennisov
(To Touchine as they return—but heard by André) It's not always officers of The Headquarters who make famous Soldiers. Yes, old boy, my Hussars were on the very extremity of the right flank—Facing Saint Cyr's dragoons. What an attack! What resistance, too.—Oh, the furor of battle. If you had seen us throw ourselves in to the cross roads, clearing to the right and left striking opposite and to the side—if you'd seen the shreds of flesh torn by my saber! If you had seen—

André
It's the affair at Bielago you are telling about, I believe. You were there?

Dennisov
Yes, I was there.

André
Yes, there are many accounts about that affair.

Dennisov
Indeed—many accounts. But those who were there have the right to speak of it—rather than the dandy—of the Headquarters who receive the decorations without having received the blows.

André
I belong to the Headquarters you are speaking of—

Dennisov
I am not speaking of you. As for you, I don't know you—and I have no desire to know you—I am speaking generally of The Headquarters—

André
But by speaking this you mean to offend me—And the thing is very simple—if you have no respect for others—you have none for yourself—

Dennisov
Ah, why—

André
Ah!—why—confess that the time and place are ill chosen for this. Soon we will all be involved in a more serious—greater duel. And for my part, I declare to you—that I consider myself in no way—untouched by your words, and that my advice is let this affair go without consequences! Still, you know where to find me!

Touchine
Attention gentlemen! I announce their Excellencies The Hof-Kriegs Wurstschnapsrath.

(Enter German Generals followed by Berg)

1st General
Der Krieg musss in Raum verlegt werden.

2nd General
Oh, Ja. Der Zweck ist nach den feind zu schwachen, so Kannn man gewiss nicht der Verlust der privat personnen in Achtung nehmen.

Berg
Oh, ja.

(They leave)

André
(Raging) Ja—In Raun verlegen. Ja, Raum—

Dennisov
Der Kreig Privat personnen—ah—these Germans of bad omen.

André
They allowed all Europe to be taken—and now they've come to teach us a lesson.

Dennisov
A fine lesson which consists in always retreating—to retreat with plucky lads like ours! And with all, they're all the rage.

Touchine
They get everything. You don't know what this Ermoloff has asked the Emperor for by way of an advance? To be promoted but in German.

Dennisov
I wouldn't have that rank.

(To André) Listen, Prince! I was wrong just now. But you know, in the army there are stupidities one repeats without knowing why—stupid prejudices. And the question is not of knowing if one belongs to such and such a corps or another—to The Headquarters or to the troops. It's to know if one is Russian, if a Russian heart beats under the uniform whatever that uniform may be.—Prince—would you give me your hand?

André
Gladly, Commander.

Touchine
Long live the great Russian army.

(They take leave of each other, shaking hands)

André
We will have an opportunity to see each other again before long! (They separate)

(Pierre enters hesitantly as if seeking his way. He wears a white bonnet, and a green coat and his glasses)

Petrov
(Seeing him, to his Comrades) Come have a look—it's worth the trouble.

Fedotov
(Running in) What the devil's that?

Makeev
Not a Soldier, for sure. he's too fat.

Petrov
Ah, say there who are you? A doctor?

Pierre
I'm an officer in the militia.

Fedotov
Yes, they can wear glasses in the militia. And what's your name?

Pierre
Piotr Kirilovitch.

Makeev
Well—Piotr Kirilovitch. What do you want? (André appears, watching, smiling)

Pierre
I'm looking for Prince André—Bolkonski.

Fedotov
The Colonel from Headquarters.

Pierre
That's it.

Makeev
He's my friend.

Petrov
Oh—in that case, you're a gentleman.

André
(Coming forward) Count Bezhoukov—Greetings to Your Excellency—

(The soldiers move away)

Petrov
Oh—He's a nobleman—and a fat nobleman at that.

André
(Hugging Pierre) My good Pierre—What's Your Excellency come to do here?

Pierre
I came like this. To present my regiment. And besides, because I've had enough of being useless.

André
You want to fight! What are you going to tell your brothers, the Free Masons?

Pierre
Don't joke my friend—I am very unfortunate—

André
My friend.

Pierre
Yes—the truth is I came here because I need to get away—escape from my life. Your life is organized since your engagement. (Reaction by André) But what's my life? I've taken my wife back. She told me she was innocent, that she was ill from my abandonment. She got her mother to tell me.

André
Yes—I heard. You still love her.

Pierre
No—I forgave her because I must bear my cross—because I had no right to refuse what she asked for—a helping hand. Besides, what did I have to pardon her for? Who's in the right down here? No one was guilty—At least she wasn't.

André
Now, there's fine reasoning. You still love her.

Pierre
I repeat to you, not at all. I received her again as my wife but I am her husband only in name. We are living separated. She doesn't suffer from it, I think she is happier being more free. She has her sister. She goes for fashion. She's never loved anything but her own body and she is the most stupid woman on earth—she seems in society—the fulfillment of wit and cleverness. then, as for me, I am the husband of this marvel! And moreover, chamberlain in retreat. I've resumed my life and the tastes of my youth. I've returned to the club. I give bachelor parties or go to them—and after my second bottle of Margaux, I find everything is very fine. Yes, a beautiful party that the Countess Helene Bezhoukov who now receives favors from a very high personage, has felt necessary to criticize—on behalf of His Highness! And I want to cut myself free of all this, and that's why I came. Already I breath better here. I see you again, I see my old friend again, and at the same time men all new to me, men who, possibly fated to die tomorrow, busy themselves with the shape of my hat. Perhaps here, there's the possibility of doing something useful, of being employed, of sacrificing oneself.

André
I really fear you won't find what you are looking for here. Everything is so strange, and so implausible compared to what one has the right to hope for. You see here a national spirit that's admirable—soldiers here who refuse Brandy before going to fight; men who put on a white shirt in the morning to die properly. And all this headed or rather thwarted by foreign officers who have admirable strategic combinations but which lack that which gives victory: the simple resolve to conquer to save the country.

Pierre
But still there is a science of strategy, military genius. War—is—it's a chess game.

André
Yes, with lots of unforeseen things. There is no science, there is no military genius. In war nothing happens that was expected—the wisest measures are denied by events; never does victory follow the plan outlined for it. But it's necessary indeed to justify the crosses, the bars, the fealties, the field-marshals' batons and they delay us, they are used in marches and countermarches to follow the fine conceptions of these gentlemen; only at length they recognize the futility of the effort and then they get exactly where you are—at disenchantment.

Pierre
But you, once the campaign is over, you have a future.

André
Ah, my friend, the future. I ask myself if I won't bless the bullet which carries me off. What misery it wouldn't preserve me from.

Pierre
Look, look, your fiancée—an adorable your girl—who loves you—

André
Who loves me! Ah, yes, you affirmed it to me—an ideal love, guaranteed—which must preserve her fidelity during an entire year of absence. You are a good lad - But if you saw the poor letters she sends me. You'd fell she's bored writing them—it's a troublesome task. She must make a fuss so her mother corrects them..

Pierre
Why Natasha is very excitable, too much herself, to express it all in one letter. I am sure that she's suffering cruelly from your absence—but she's not the girl to put her tears on paper.

André
She suffers! She doesn't seem to. If sometimes, some enthusiasm pierces through these letters it's for your wife—The Countess Helene—and her brilliant company.

Pierre
Yes—I know—Although I do not concern myself with the company of The Countess, I do know that Natasha sees her often. But I was unaware that things had come to this. And I regret it, because it's not worthy of my little friend. This world is so strange. Where one knows neither what is good nor what is bad, nor who is wise nor who is crazy.

André
Ah, my friend do you know a world where one knows it? Wisdom—I believe is only thus, it's enthusiasm, joy in doing what one does without knowing why—but because one loves doing it. And these are our true wise men—your friend Nicholas—your godson Petia.

(Enter Nicholas and Petia followed by the Cossack Komarov and young Vincent Bosse—a little French drummer boy)

Petia
Come on, Komarov—lead the prisoners to the barracks—(To Vincent Bosse) And you, my lad, move faster. When you are resting there you look at me with your moronic eyes

(To Komarov who grabs the little boy roughly) Not so rough, will you, you're going to hurt him.

(Komarov leaves with the little drummer boy)

Nicholas
(Seeing Pierre) Count Bezhoukov.

Petia
My Colonel. Are you coming to place yourself at the head of your regiment?

Pierre
Oh, no—I merely came. But since I can hug you, I am quite happy to be here.

André
(To Petia) And as for me—I am not vexed to see you again my young friend?

Nicholas
Yes! He's a bit off his head, the kid….

Petia
Ah, I advise you to speak—you did such fine stuff at Smolensk.

Nicholas
Well! And you—when, instead of going to your post by the covered way in accordance with the general's orders, you went under fire—completely under French fire and twice, facing the enemy you discharged your pistol. The General was furious.

Petia
Bah! The General is a dirty German—he understands nothing of Russian ways.

André
Russian ways mustn't be to get oneself killed for nothing.

Pierre
Petia, my child, think of those who love you!

Petia
Oh—Colonel! No danger! It's very amusing! No danger—

Nicholas
Well! And your last escapade! The idea of going to take a prisoner from the forward posts.

André
Prisoners again! There's no use taking prisoners.

Pierre
Oh—why, that would be barbaric.

André
Quite to the contrary. War would be shorter, and consequently, less cruel—War is not a gracious thing, but the most villainous activity—it must be understood and not made into a game.

Pierre
That's not a reason to divest oneself of all feeling!

André
Ah—I know that feeling. It's that of a woman who feels ill when she sees a young calf killed. She's so nice that she cannot see the blood, but she eats veal with a good appetite when it's covered with sauce. Besides, it doesn't save anyone by making prisoners—in a convoy of a hundred men—hardly thirty will make it. Men die of hunger or are killed—In that case it's better to get it over with right away.

Petia
(Aside, looking uneasily toward the barracks) Ah—if I weren't afraid they'd say it's a kid who pities another kid.

André
(Noticing) Ah, you're looking around for your prisoner. He interests you.

Petia
Colonel—

André
(Smiling) Come on! (To Komarov who returns) Go find the little French drummer.

(Komarov leaves)

Petia
(Hugging André) Oh you are nice! And I love you a lot! (Embraces him)

André
That's good! That's good! (Distant roll of drums, trumpets, shouting)

André
Ah—General Koutouzov has returned to camp—Come with me, Pierre—

Pierre
(Leaving, to Petia) Till later, my little friend.

Petia
Right, my good father.

Nicholas
(To Petia) As for me, I'm going back to my duty.

(He leaves, Komarov and Bosse enter)

Petia
What could I really do for him?

Komarov
Here's the good fellow, your lordship. He's a brave lad.

Petia
(Timidly) Come on! Come! Don't be afraid. No one will harm you— (He touches his hand)

Vincent Bosse
Thanks, Sir.

Petia
Are you hungry? (To Komarov) Has he been given food?

Komarov
Oh—he's well cared for, your Lordship. He's a brave lad. Ah, he was hungry like a wolf.

Petia
(To Vincent Bosse) You are—from Paris?

Vincent
No, Sir, I am from Tours.

Petia
Ah—is it a big town?

Vincent Bosse
Oh, yes, Sir—it's beautiful.

Petia
You have a family?

Vincent Bosse
I had two brothers but they've been killed. I have only Mama.

Petia
What does your Mama do?

Vincent Bosse
She's a seamstress.

Petia
Ah. (Vexed he fumbles in his pockets and pulls out some money that he gives to Bosse) Take this. It's for your mother.

Vincent Bosse
Ah! Monsieur—How good you are! As for me, I thought you were an enemy—

Petia
Goodbye, my friend—I will take care of you.

Vincent Bosse
But! Sir! The prisoners say they are going to move us—they're going to form a convoy of 100 men.

(Sound of trumpets)

Komarov
Your Lordship, it's the signal for departure. They are calling the prisoners. I have to bring the child. He has to leave with the others.

Vincent Bosse
Goodbye, then, Sir—(Going to leave)

Petia
(Aside) No! He won't go. (Calling) Komarov. Give me your Cloak.

(He puts it on Vincent's shoulders) I will keep you with me. You will stay in my detachment!

Vincent Bosse
Ah, sir, thanks—

Petia
Poor little fellow. It would have been a shame.

(Petia leaves with Bosse. Komarov withdraws)

(Dolokhov and Anatole enter)

Dolokhov
Now this is amusing, new. And it's sweet of you to come tell it to the poor soldier Dolokhov.

Anatole
I won't hide it from you old boy. I need you—it's for that I came express.

Dolokhov
Ah, ah—we are plotting some evil deed. And my old experience. But tell me, tell me, will you? Then this little Natasha!

Anatole
I am mad for her. And without boasting, I think that on her part—

Dolokhov
Ah—you won't miss one of 'em—with your handsome, guileless face. But still—this one—the fiancée of Prince Bolkonski. Aren't you exaggerating the power of your charms?

Anatole
I'm certain of my business—I've been sure of it since our first meeting at the theater. The evening that my sister Helene presented me—

Dolokhov
Ah, the sweet sister is in it—that dear Countess—

Anatole
Ah, yes—she's been sweet to me in all this. She gave a delightful evening party and she contrived for me with her delicate woman-of-the-world touch: —a moment alone with Natasha!

Dolokhov
And Natasha said the great word.

Anatole
No! But I saw the unease my kiss caused her—

Dolokhov
And then—

Anatole
And then I'm going to carry her off.

Dolokhov
Oh—big trouble, rape, courts, family, scandal.

Anatole
Ah, my dear, I've got to have her. She's a morsel to savor—those arms, those shoulders

Dolokhov
Less beautiful than your sister, still—

Anatole
Oh—another thing—And a little foot—hair—that entices you.

Dolokhov
Yes, you're an amateur.

Anatole
Ah—What do you want? As for me, I only love women. I do harm to no one. I don't stoop beneath my noble rank. I live decently, my conscience is pure. So, I've really got the right to amuse myself.

Dolokhov
Yes—you'll be forgiven a lot because you've loved a lot, Rascal—But this one—wait till she's married.

Anatole
Oh—you know me, I adore virgins.

Dolokhov
Yes, I know it—you've already had a misfortune with a little girl.

Anatole
Alas, but these are misfortunes which do not occur—twice. And I came to seek you—

Dolokhov
Well, and the service?

Anatole
This will be a matter of service—I will demand you as an escort.

Dolokhov
Ah—But I have no desire to miss the battle.

Anatole
But you will return. Wouldn't it be amusing to croak three or four horses?

Dolokhov
What would be amusing would be to play a nice trick on the noble Prince André and on this good fat Pierre. Well, since you wish it, I am your man—

Anatole.
You are my true friend.

Dolokhov
We'll need money—20,000 roubles.

Anatole
My sister will give me 10,000. For the rest, my brother-in-law Bezhoukov....

Dolokhov
Or if necessary, we will bleed a Jew—count on me. I will justify your confidence. I will furnish you everything—the coachman—I have Balaga—an admirable man for these sorts of affairs. A defrocked priest to bless the ceremony with two witnesses at two thousand a piece, the passport and finally the love letter which will throw the little Countess palpitating into your arms. Ah, I know how to carry 'em off—Come on—you need only have me attached to your person—

Anatole
Ah, my Dolokhov—you are a brave heart. I will return the favor, you will see.

Dolokhov
(Jokingly assuming military posture) I am at the orders of Your High Excellency.

(Shouting off)—Koutouzov! Koutouzov! (Makeev and Zikine run in shouting) Koutouzov! Koutouzov!

Petrov
What is it they are braying about? What's going on?

Zikine
Something great, comrades, something great. We've got him Koutouzov is nominated. He's our leader.

All
Hurrah for Koutouzov!

Dolokhov
What are they saying?

Anatole
The truth. The old debauchee is Generalissimo.

Dolokhov.
And you didn't say anything to me about it. Ah, indeed, that's admirable for goodness sakes!

Anatole
My God, I wasn't thinking about it. I confess my pretty Natasha was occupying me more than the one-eyed Koutouzov.

Dolokhov
Ah, you are too much! Koutouzov Generalissimo—finally it's there.

Anatole
Oh—The Emperor didn't do it willingly—he had to give in to public opinion.

Zikine
Say, will you. This news is certain at least?

Makeev
As certain as you are merely a young calf. The Tsar, who knows all our thoughts said to himself something like this, "All my brave children demand Koutouzov for a father—Well," he said to his minister of war—"We must give him to them. Pass me a paper to sign" He signed—and there you are—Long live Koutouzov!

Petrov
This is going to be fortunate. Biscuits, meat, we're going to have everything. And enough tobacco to make you sick.

Bikov
So much the better, at least as you won't borrow mine.

Makeev
Ah, things will go better than with the sausage makers—By the way do you have merely a rope to tie up Napoleon?

Petrov
Ah! Napoleon's already in flight and we've got the whole French army—

(Sings) Ah what glory we shall have, what victories we'll win with Koutouzov, our father.

(The soldiers repeat in chorus. In the midst of acclamations, Koutouzov accompanied by André, Pierre, Berg, the Commandant, Generals and a brilliant Headquarters staff enter)

Koutouzov
Thanks, gentlemen, thanks. Your acclamations touch me almost to tears.

Makeev
It's actually true he's crying.

Koutouzov
We will try to do good work. Our guests have been with us too long already—The times come to escort them out.

All
Hurrah!

Koutouzov
Yes, great times. To the point which they've led us. God willing. (A pause then addressing Pierre) Count, you came to breathe the

smell of gun powder? Agreeable isn't it? I have the honor to be adorer of Madame, your spouse—Her health?

Pierre
Perfect, Excellency—

Koutouzov
Just like her beauty. Ah, Bolkonski. Hello, Prince you know that the son of Bolkonski is my son—You will remain with me.

André
Thanks to Your Excellency—and gladly—But I fear being unable to render great service in Headquarters—I would like to fight in the ranks.

Touchine
Ah, Prince—you are a real soldier.

André
Excuse me, Excellency, if I refuse the honor of being close to you.

Koutouzov
I regret it. You would be necessary to me. But you are right. These are always plenty of staff officers—but men like you. Ah, I haven't forgotten your conduct at Austerlitz, the flag captured by a young Prince—Follow your route, my son. I know that it's the path of honor. But come kiss me—you'll deliver this kiss to your father.

André
(Rushing into Koutouzov's arms) Ah, Excellency!

Berg
(To Pierre) Count, could I ask you to present me to the Serenissimo?

Pierre
(To Berg) Why, Colonel Berg—

Berg
No—Commander only. The Prince has just refused entry to the Marshall's staff and I—although I have the post of aide to the Head of the Headquarters on the left flank of the infantry of the First Army—a very pleasant situation and very much in sight—I would gladly leave it to be close to the Serenissimo.

Pierre
But the Serenissimo seems busy.

Berg
Oh—he's so well disposed to Count Bezhoukov—

Pierre
Your High Excellency would allow me to present to him—Col—Commandant Berg—

Berg
Commandant Berg—aide to the leader of the Headquarters staff of the left flank of the First Army, wounded at Smolensk—

Koutouzov
It seems you did well. You are fat and rosy but (seeing Commandant Touchine) now here's one who was more seriously hurt, he's an old soldier of Brunau, of Ismail. How's it going, comrade? Still that little weakness for Bacchus! Men are not perfect and you are a brave one.

(To His Staff) And you, gang—Ready to do well, right? Heavens, that one—what's he doing, looking at me?

Commandant
Excellency, it's Dolokhov, degraded as a result of—

Koutouzov
Ah, yes, Dolokhov—I know the scandal. Well, I hope this lesson will suffice you. Serve well: the Emperor is merciful and I won't forget you—if you are deserving.

Dolokhov
I ask only one thing of Your High Excellency—it's to give me the opportunity to efface my fault and to prove my devotion to the Emperor and the country.

Koutouzov
Good, good—I know all the phrases you can say to me. Thanks to all—and a double ration of brandy to all the troops.

Zikine
A double ration. Now that's a leader! (Singing with his comrades) Ah what glory we shall have, what victories we'll win—with Koutouzov, our father.

(Koutouzov and his staff leave)

General
(To Dolokhov) You heard at the first affair—officer's bars!

(Dolokhov salutes with an expression of ironic respect)

Dennisov
(Pursuing Lavrouchka) Ah, cussed Lavrouchka. Devil doll—I'll beat you up when I catch you.

Nicholas
What's he done to you?

Dennisov
Ah, Rostov, you don't know? The purse that I gave you—you put it where I told you?

Nicholas
Yes—under the pillow—Well?

Dennisov
Well, it's no longer there.

Nicholas
It's no longer there?

Dennisov
I am quite sure.

Lavrouchka
Oh, you are sure. It's always the same—you throw things in the first corner and then you forget where— Look in your pockets.

Nicholas
No, I am sure, too. I even made the remark that you would have your money under your pillow like the portrait of a mistress.

Dennisov
Well, that purse must be found.

Nicholas
(Looking at Dennisov searchingly) Indeed it must.

Dennisov
(To Lavrouchka) You are going to return to look for it again. And if you don't find it you will pay its worth on your shoulders.

Lavrouchka
It's not my fault if it disappeared—I ask myself a little—how?—for goodness sakes. No one came to the tent except Count Rostov and the Lieutenant.

Nicholas
What Lieutenant?

Lavrouchka
Lieutenant Telianine.

Dennisov
I sent him to wait for me in our tent. The colonel had sent for me.

(To Lavrouchka) Come on, you go look for it, and bring it! Yes bring it. (Shaking him) Or if not—

Nicholas
Dennisov! Release him! I know who took the purse.

Dennisov
You know? Oh, no, it's impossible! It's crazy, you've gone mad. Ah—I won't allow it. The purse is in the tent, and Lavrouchka—

Nicholas
I know who took it, and I am going—let me take care of it.

Dennisov
And as for me, I tell you do nothing at all.

Nicholas
Ah, but, ah, but—Do you understand what you are saying. I'm the one you ordered to take the purse—and Telianine alone went into the tent. So if it's not him, it's—Ah—let me alone—(Noticing Telianine) Oh—God is good—He's sending him to me—

Dennisov
(Distancing himself) Ah—may the devil take you.

Telianine
(Heading toward the tent of the Headquarters staff) General's order—

Sergeant
General's not here.

Telianine
It wasn't worth the trouble of hurrying here. So be it. I'll wait. (Sits at cantina. To waiter) A glass of Kvass.

Waiter
Yes, Lieutenant.

(Nicholas comes to sit on a bench beside Telianine)

Telianine
(Repressing a reaction of vexation) Ah, you've returned here, my Commandant!

Nicholas
(Annoyed) Yes, yes—As you see.

Telianine
Would you allow me to offer you—

Nicholas
No, no! Thanks.

Telianine
In that case, I'm leaving. I'm in a bit of a hurry. Waiter.

(He takes out the purse but carefully hides it under the table. He tosses a coin on the table)

Nicholas
(Rising) (Aside) A new coin. (Aloud) Lieutenant, would you allow me to examine that purse—

Telianine
That purse! You noticed it. It's indeed a pretty enough purse. Pretty enough!

Nicholas
Give it to me! Will you—?

Telianine
Why yes, gladly. Look at it at your leisure.

Nicholas
(Taking the purse) Thanks.

Telianine
In war one is really forced to make economies—But as we've arrived in garrison this purse will soon be dry—poor purse. Well commandant return it to me. I am expected. (Silence by Nicholas)

Yes, opposite at Headquarters staff. Come on, return me my purse.

Nicholas
Your purse.

Telianine
Well, yes, my purse. What's wrong with you to look at me like that—?

Nicholas
(Grasping his arms, very low) It's Dennisov's purse and his money—(In his ear) How much have you taken!

Telianine
What! What! How dare you—I—I—it's necessary to have an explanation.

Nicholas
I know what I'm saying and I will prove it.

Telianine
Me? Me?—I –?

Nicholas
Yes, you—

Telianine
Ah, Count. Don't ruin a young man—here's this cursed money! Take it—(He throws the purse on the table) I have an old father—a mother—

Nicholas
(Taking the purse and starting to leave) Wretch! How were you able to do that??

(Telianine tries to kiss his hand)

Nicholas
Ah! Don't touch me—(To Dennisov who returned) Hold on—here's your purse.

Dennisov
(To Telianine) If you have need of this money, keep it.

(He throws the purse on the table. Petrov and Sergeant enter heading toward the Headquarters staff from which a general emerges)

Sergeant
(To General) General. They caught that soldier Fedotov, from the second company, in the act of pilfering in the camp. What must be done to him?

(In front of the General, Dennisov, Nicholas and Telianine have assumed a military bearing)

General
What must be done? Why what is done to thieves—Why whip him and lock him up.

(Sergeant and Petrov leave)

And let this serve as an example the rest of you—remember that the first duty of a soldier is to be an honest man. All thieves are unworthy of belonging to the army.

(Screams off of soldier being punished)

Telianine
(Stifling a scream and bending his back as if receiving a blow) Ah!

General
Fine. The scars will remain and be noticed, the blackguard.

CURTAIN

ACT IV

Scene 6

A boudoir in the Bezhoukov Palace in Petersburg.

Mlle Berthe
(To Natasha who's looking in a mirror) I assure Mademoiselle, that it's the greatest novelty!

Helene
(Entering) Why yes—the dress is pretty—And she who is wearing it is charming.

Natasha
Oh—Countess—How nice that is of you.

Helene
I'm coming to admire you, my sweet—it's because she's pretty like no one else. (Hugs her) Hello, Mademoiselle Berthe .

Mlle Berthe
Hello, Madame Countess.

Helene
Finally, they brought you a mirror—this brave Count had installed you so ill. He knows so little about what ladies like.

Natasha
Oh—we are admirably nice. Our good friend Pierre has done so many nice things for our stay in Petersburg.

Helene
Ah, by the way, I just met Maria Dmitrievna—but the "terrible dragon" didn't seem to notice me. Is she staying a long while in Petersburg?

Natasha
Oh, no. She's returning to Moscow tomorrow!

Helene
Why, let's see these marvels. Oh—the very latest type. Truly there's only Oberchalmet for dressing in the Parisian taste. She's finally made me a dress of metallic gauze. You must absolutely have one like it.

(To Mlle Berthe) See to it, Miss Berthe.

Mlle Berthe
At Madame's orders.

(She leaves)

Helene
Yes, that's charming. We seem like two sisters, me the older—

Natasha
Oh, Madame, if I could look like you—

Helene
Why my darling, Anatole himself who still spoils me wasn't able to hide it from me. Ah—you can boast of having made a victim. I've never seen him like this. He's mad, crazy mad over you, my dear.

Natasha
Ah, Countess!

Helene
How she blushes, my delight. But because you're engaged to Prince Bolkonski is no reason that others should be prevented from showing you their admiration. Why do you have those eyes? I hope you are not going to make a ruin of yourself. Prince André knows the world despite his cold airs—which give a chill, and he would be the first to advise you to live according to your rank. I am sure that a bourgeois happiness—completely intimate—would not enchant him much. He's not capable, I think, of those great feelings, of those reactions of the soul that a man no longer sees except in a woman of the world. As for example my poor Anatole! For you brought him here. I don't make him better than he is—and surely he has had in our world—lots of conquests—it's understood—they say Mlle Georges— Amusing, isn't it? But since he's seen you, how transformed he's been. He makes himself unhappy and it's for you alone—Show him at

least some gratitude. Be pitying—for a folly which is so understandable.

Natasha
But if he truly has feeling for me it would be very wrong to encourage him.

Helene
What a Muscovite you are! Why no, my delight! You mustn't see things in a tragic light. You need to laugh and amuse yourself in life! Without harming anyone. Come on, my darling, meditate on my moral—give my tenderness to your family and see you soon.

(They kiss, Helene leaves) (Pause)

Chambermaid
(Entering mysteriously) Miss is Alone?

Natasha
What do you want?

Chambermaid
A man directed me to deliver this to you (She offers a letter) Only, in the name of Christ, don't let anyone know.

Natasha
Let me have it. That's fine. Go! (The Chambermaid leaves) It's from him! From him!

(Reading) "Since yesterday, my fate is decided.—to be loved by you or die. I have no other way out! Certain mysterious obstacles, that I can explain only to you seem to oppose our happiness! But say a word, just one—"yes"—and all the obstacles will be removed! My future, my fortune, my life—I place them all at your feet, all I want in the world is you—and without you I am dying. If you love me, no human force will prevent us from being happy—I will carry you to the end of the earth and love will be the conqueror!" A word—just one—yes, and love is conqueror—What's happening in me—where am I?

(Sonia enters) You, Sonia.

Sonia
Yes, my darling—I startled you? You were dreaming?—What's the matter?

Natasha
Me—nothing—

Sonia
Why yes—you are no longer the same—you have a mysterious manner—some strange things are going on. I saw a chambermaid who fled at my approach—what's all this mean? You know very well we've never hidden anything from each other. Speak, my Natasha, speak.

Natasha
(Throwing herself in her arms) My Sonia.

Sonia
Say something, will you?

Natasha
Yes, I must tell you all my happiness.

Sonia
But I know it. Prince Bolkonski your fiancée loves you.

Natasha
No, that wasn't love! You don't suspect what love is.

Sonia
(Morosely) You think—and Nicholas—

Natasha
You don't love him—

Sonia
I don't love him?

Natasha
No question, since you were able to give him up! And as for me—Neither did I know love before having met the one who is everything for me.

Sonia
The one who is everything for you? Could it be? Yes—I thought I noticed that Anatole Kouraguine—

Natasha
Yes, he's the one I adore!

Sonia
But it's madness! You've only seen him three or four times.

Natasha
It seems to me I've loved him for a hundred years, that I've never loved anybody before him—you cannot understand, Sonia—(She hugs her) As soon as I noticed him, I felt that he was my master, that I was his slave—that I couldn't help but love him—yes, his slave! Let him command, I will obey—

Sonia
Why this is madness! Think what you are saying!

Natasha
I am thinking only of him. I love him!

Sonia
What about him? Are you really sure he loves you?

Natasha
Him? Does he love me?—oh, my poor Sonia.

Sonia
You know they say many things about the handsome Anatole! And not very pretty ones. I've heard Papa and Mama talk of them. They say he pays court to all the ladies, but that he has no heart. If this were only a caprice, my darling!

Natasha
(Stung) A caprice! Truly! A caprice!

Sonia
In the end, what proof have you?

Natasha
What proof?

Sonia
You are really pretty, my Natasha. But if, in the end he has no heart?.

Natasha
No heart! What proof? What proof? Here, read this.

Sonia
What's this?

Natasha
A letter which you must have seen brought to me since you are spying on me—

Sonia
Oh—don't be naughty with your Sonia? What! You opened this letter?! You read it! You've got an intrigue! You, you!

Natasha
Why read it, read it will you.

Sonia
(Reading) Yes, yes, I see!

Natasha
He gives me his life! Everything! He wants to die—And he doesn't love me!

Sonia
Who knows! If he's a deceiver—if he says as much to all women.

Natasha
To all women! Oh—get out! Get out!

Sonia
What do these mysterious reasons, these obstacles, mean?

Natasha
Eh! I don't know. But he'll triumph over them. He's the most noble of men.

Sonia
It's not a question of nobility. He must address himself to your father! Your father, Natasha—aren't you thinking of that? And what about Nicholas when he finds out?

Natasha
Why, you want me to die! I cannot live without him, you hear? I need someone. I love no one but him. Sonia, Go away I don't want to be angry with you. But go away. In the name of God, go away! You see plainly how you are torturing me.

Sonia
Natasha, I'm afraid for you.

Natasha
You are too good!

Sonia
I'm afraid you'll ruin yourself!

Natasha
I'll ruin myself! I'll ruin myself! I'll ruin myself! And as quickly as possible! It's not your affair! Not yours, not anybody's. Leave me alone! Leave me alone! I hate you.

Sonia
Natasha!

Natasha
I hate you! I hate you! And you are my enemy, my enemy forever!

Sonia
Well as for me, I love you, and I intend to save you. Promise me that you won't say that abominable word again!

Natasha
I am ready to give him my life.

Sonia
My God! My God! Who to go to? (With sudden inspiration) I will save you despite yourself. I know quite well how to prevent your dishonor.

(She leaves)

Natasha
(Alone, dreamily) Dishonor (A gentle rap on the door) Oh I'm afraid—No—don't come in.

(The door opens: Anatole enters admitted by the chambermaid. He casts a sable cloak on the chair)

Anatole
Yes. It's me, coming to seek the word on which my life depends.

Natasha
No, no, leave! I am affianced; I cannot love you! I must belong to another, I already do.

Anatole
No, no—you are mine and mine alone and forever! You haven't the right to reject me. I've left everything, broken everything behind me. I no longer have family or friends: you are my only consolation, my only future! Come!

Natasha
Leave! Leave my father? Never!

Anatole
Don't push me to despair. We can be so happy! You will be my wife! A priest is waiting for us. You will be my wife before God! My wife. A whole life of intoxication!

Natasha
(Weakly) No, no—from pity!

Anatole
Oh—I have the joys of paradise before me! And I'll let them escape me! Ah! (He wraps her in his sable cloak) Come, adorable girl! Come! I'm carrying my happiness in my arms! (He picks up Natasha and heads towards the door)

Maria Dmitrievna
(Appears with Sonia; Sonia vanishes) Stop thief! And put down your booty! (Anatole recoils terrified) Leave this child alone. So it was for this you returned from the army? So this is how you fight!

(To Natasha who's got fire) And you, slut! You, shameless— You are behaving like the worst of women.

Anatole
(Grabbing Natasha by the waist) Leave us alone! Let us pass!

Maria Dmitrievna
(Separating them) No, my lad! I am here! And your trick failed.

(Voices of Dolokhov who shouts in the street. "Kouraguine! Treachery! Flee! Return!") You hear? Your accomplices also have been nabbed!

Pierre
(Enters hurriedly) So it was actually true! Poor little girl.

Maria Dmitrievna
Ah, you! Pierre. What's happened?

Pierre
The traitors are betrayed.

Natasha
(Collapsing in an armchair) I'm going to die.

Pierre
Poor little thing.

Maria Dmitrievna
(To Anatole who tries to sneak out) Ah, you're leaving without asking for your due. You came to bring shame here, and you—

Pierre
Leave it to me, Maria Dmitrievna. It's to me that Prince Anatole Kouraguine owes an explanation.

Anatole
Why, sir—what have you come here to do?

Pierre
And you? What did you come here to do?

Anatole
I don't believe I'm obliged to answer questions put in that tone.

Pierre
Ah, why, coward. Ah, why, drunkard—You must answer me. (Takes him by the collar) Oh, I'm going to strangle you like a nasty animal.

(He shakes him so violently by the collar that Anatole's clothes are torn)

Natasha
Oh, Pierre, he's the most noble of men.

(An imperative gesture by Maria Dmitrievna imposing silence on Natasha)

Anatole
Come on! Come on! It's idiotic! Look at these manners.

Helene
(Entering) Why what's going on? What are you doing to my poor Anatole? This is a scandal.

Pierre
A scandal indeed! And it's your work! Wherever you go there's corruption and evil.

Helene
Count! You are forgetting that your house is mine. And if you forget yourself in my home.

Pierre
Ah—Go put on your grand airs elsewhere, and leave me here to deal with this.

(Returning to Anatole) Wretch!—No, I won't be violent! Don't worry! Two things. First of all, tomorrow you will leave Petersburg—

Anatole
But how can I—?

Pierre
Secondly! You will never say a word of what happened between you and Natasha Rostov.

Anatole
But—

Pierre
Try to understand that these are honest men and honest women, that you are forbidden to amuse yourself with by ruining their lives—Amuse yourself with certain women like (Gesturing towards Helene) With them you are within your rights—they know what you want from them! But respect the others! If you don't, you will find those who will demand satisfaction.

Helene
Anatole! You cannot endure—

Anatole
No—surely! You've said words to me—that in my capacity as a man of honor—I shall not allow anyone to—

Pierre
What do you want?

Anatole
I want—

Pierre
Satisfaction, perhaps—

Anatole
Yes—I want you to retract your words—ah—but—if you want me to accept your conditions—ah, but....

Pierre
I retract them! I retract them! If that's all. And I'll even give you money for your expenses.

Anatole
(With a sort of smile) Count, I have only one word! I will leave!

Pierre
Go where you like! To Poland near your wife, if you like—

Helene
(Trying to silence Pierre) Count!

(Natasha rises and listens anxiously)

Pierre
Because you are married, you who go about carrying off young girls. Oh really, despite yourself—but a father that you outraged as you intended to outrage Count Rostov forced you to marry his daughter!

(Scream from Natasha)

Helene
What you are doing is unworthy of a gallant man, Count! Come brother! Let's leave the gentleman to his brutalities.

(They leave)

Pierre
Cowardly and heartless family.

Maria Dmitrievna
Good, Pierre. You spoke as you had to.

Sonia
(Enters running) Papa! Papa! He's just come back.

Maria Dmitrievna
Come on. Stand up wicked girl. Stand up and greet the Count well. Do you want to kill your father now? (Changing tone) Come on. Courage, my little Cossack.

Pierre
Yes, courage, Natasha.

Count Rostov
(Entering happily) Ah, what a nice surprise! Pierre, Maria Dmitrievna. Why it's a day of joy. Hello Sonia! Well, Natasha. No one's coming to hug me.

Natasha
Father—

Count Rostov
Why what's wrong, my angel? You are all pale? You've been crying.

Natasha
Nothing, father, nothing.

Maria Dmitrievna
It's nothing! Stupid young girl! It will pass.

CURTAIN

ACT IV

Scene 7

Borodino

A portion of land overlooking the battlefield. The night of carnage. Piles of dead and wounded. Cannon in the distance. Moans; among the wounded, André and Anatole.

Koutouzov
(With two Aides de Camp) Hum! Lots of people on the ground. But down there by Borodino, there are a lot more. The eagle got it in the wing. Ah, I cannot take it anymore. Have them serve me some little thing here.

(They set up a meal on a drum)

Aide de Camp
Your Highness! General Volsogen.

Koutouzov
Ah! Ah!—Military instructor—great German school. Im Raum verlegen!

Volsogen
(To his ordinance officers) Oh! Oh—the old gentleman's putting himself completely at his ease (Coming closer and barely touching his hat) I excuse myself for interrupting you during your meal, Excellency—but I must on the behalf of General Barclay de Tolly, warn you of the situation on the left flank. All the points of our position are in the hands of the enemy. Taking them back is impossible, because—because there are no more troops. They fled and no one knew how to stop them.

Koutouzov
(Stops eating and looks at him in astonishment) What are you telling me?

Volsogen
I don't think I have the right to hide from Your Excellency what I have seen—the troops are completely disorganized.

Koutouzov
(Rising, frowning, and striding toward Volsogen) You've seen, you've seen! How—how dare you, (Threatening gesture with his trembling hand) How dare you, sir, say that to me. You saw, saw ill, sir, and you know nothing about it. Say on my behalf to General Barclay that his information is false—and that I, The Commanding General, I know better than he—the battlefield situation.

Volsogen
But, Excellency—

Koutouzov
The enemy's been pushed back on the left flank and defeated on the right. What you took for fugitives, were wounded who were taking the air. If you saw ill, sir, don't presume to say what you don't know—Please be so good as to rejoin General Barclay and to transmit to him for tomorrow the absolute order to attack the enemy. They've been pushed back everywhere. I thank God for it, and our valiant army—the enemy is defeated and tomorrow we will drive them out of Holy Russia! (Bursting into tears) Yes tomorrow, the attack, the attack—take my orders. (He leaves)

Volsogen
(Shrugging his shoulders. To his Aide) The old gentlemen's making fun. Tomorrow—retreat. Nothing but retreat is possible. We've lost half the army—and the road to Moscow's open to the French.

(They leave)

André
(Rising among the wounded, in delirium) No—no—it's a shame! What an example for the soldiers. Useless to say: Hit the ground! I won't throw myself there. Ah, the grenade rolls around One would say a smoking top. Is this death? Ah, I don't want to die. As for me, I love life—The grass, the earth, the air—I don't want it. Ah, I'm hurting. You'd say that all of it entered my side. It's over. The battle. Have they caught him?—That little brown dog

that ran in front of the ranks. The prairie is freshly cut—smells nice. Timokhine—a bullet passed—on the other side. A French officer with his face all red with blood.—the other one, in his arms. The battle. The fort. But it's all finished—everything is indifferent now. What was it like down there? What happened here. Why so many regrets about leaving life?. There's something in life I didn't understand.—something I do not understand.

(The stars rise)

How alone I am here—here—yet there are others, still—a crowd—Fine, they are dead—already gone—Oh, it's sad to be alone, to be an unknown, a stranger (Anatole moans)

A moan. That one isn't dead. Sir—An—ah, I see him—he's handsome—Why, yes, it's him—him who? Why is he here—Yes, I know him well. Yes, yes, I know him—I'm not alone. He was with me in my life—something in common between us—yes a mournful thing—mournful. Still, it's nice that he's here. But what bond is there between him and me? It's like a childhood memory. Ah, yes, coolness, a young girl, a joy—ah—she, she—all startled amazed on the road and laughing, laughing the ball—a charm that little Rostova her thin arm emerging from her red sleeve—if she goes to her cousin first, she'll be my wife—my wife! Ah, everything—I remember everything! How I loved her! The dear pretty little creature—Why it's all my life surrounding me—I am fine. It's Anatole. He's nice to be here to allow me to see everything again. I love him.

(Moan by Anatole—"Water!")

Ah, if I could get him some help!—But no, no, I cannot—poor Anatole. Natasha—what a pity! Well, it's sweet to love, to forgive—Ah—the nice warmth of heart—tears—joys—Yes, love for those who hate us—love for those who love us—yes—love that God preached on earth and that I didn't understand All understood, pardon me—because now I understand. I know the word of life—It's, It's love. (Falls down again)

(An officer appears leading Stretcher Bearers)

Officer
Ah, Ah—there are some to collect here—this way—no mistakes be careful—don't take those who are dead.

First Stretcher Bearer
How about this one. (Pointing to Anatole)

Officer
This one's dead! (Examining André) And this one's not much better.

(Groans of the wounded—The Stretcher Bearers are going to pick up a soldier. Officer's looking at André) Why it's—oh, take this one before the others—it's Prince Bolkonski.

Second Stretcher Bearer
(To his comrade) For sure, even in the next world life is better for the gentlemen.

CURTAIN

ACT V

Scene 8

A square in Moscow in front of the Palace of the Governor General— In front of the Palace—a flight of stone steps reached by a double stairway. A crowd.

First Passerby
Well! What news from Fili?

Second Passerby
Still nothing. The Council of war must have been over for a long while.

First Passerby
Oh—we have nothing to fear. They will relieve Moscow. Papa Koutouzov will know how to protect us.

Third Passerby
And what about us! We will defend ourselves until death!

First Passerby
(To Second Passerby) You've received your weapons?

Second Passerby
Yes, a rusty old lance.

First Passerby
And me, I've got a saber taken from the Kremlin.

Fourth Passerby
You won't be able to do anything with your old tools. What's needed are troops. As for me, in my three shops I've got a 100,000 roubles of merchandise. Who will guard them if the army withdraws?

A Woman
My God! My God! What's going to become of us? The French are going to massacre us all! My children! My poor children!

Bilibine
(Entering) Calm down, my brave woman! The French have never committed horrors. In Berlin, In Vienna the women were joking with them.

A Woman
Yes, but as for us, we are not Germans.

Bilibine
Anyway! good people you have nothing to fear—Governor Rostopchine is watching over you. He's preparing a balloon to set the French camp on fire. He's removing the icons.

(Religious singing—off. The crowd rushes)

A Woman
Yes, yes! Here's the procession—It's our Holy Mother the Virgin of Iverskaia.

(The crowd disperses)

Bilibine
Ah—now we are saved

(Noticing Pierre) Why, I'm not mistaken, it's Count Bezhoukov!

Pierre
(Shouting to himself) Yes—It's indeed the correct calculation . It's I who am designated—

Bilibine
Hello, Bezhoukov! What's wrong with you?

Pierre
Ah—Excuse me, my dear Bilibine. I was dreaming—happy to meet you. I'm going to Governor Rostopchine. I'm looking for news.

Bilibine
Just like me. I've taken his orders for the Chanceries—I might even say for the departure of the Chanceries—for I think I've fathomed Rostopchine's thoughts. And better, perhaps, than he

does himself. He's decided to evacuate Moscow—because Koutouzov cannot defend it.

Pierre
What! Our father Koutouzov!!!

Bilibine
Our father Koutouzov has the choice of sacrificing Moscow or risking loss of the army.

Pierre
But Moscow is the Holy Capital!

Bilibine
Fine thing to have a capital if there's no more country. And today the country is the army! You see, the only true tactic before the French is emptiness.

Pierre
Indeed, numerous indeed are the great Families who've already left or who are preparing to depart. My friends The Rostovs are in the midst of moving

Bilibine
On the subject of the Rostov's what's become of she who must be Princess Bolkonski?

Pierre
She will never be; it was only a project; it's been abandoned.

Bilibine
And you Count, what are you doing?

Pierre
Me, I'm staying.

Bilibine
You are staying to salute the great man whom I once heard you praise so magnificently.

Pierre
Not exactly! But listen—you will perhaps make fun of me, but you will be wrong. You've read the Apocalypse—of John the Prophet.

Bilibine
Not very well—

Pierre
Well—you will see in chapter XII, verse 18—that the beast—Meaning Napoleon—

Bilibine
Ah, I see you no longer admire him.

Pierre
(Continuing) Must be defeated by a man whose name, comports exactly in letters as numbers indicated in the verse having the numbers desired

Bilibine
Truly?

Pierre
And it is found counting the letters of my name "The Russian Bezhoukov"—gets exactly to the desired number. I am then the one who will kill the beast! Laugh at your ease! As for me, I'm waiting.

Bilibine
Why no, I'm not laughing, my dear friend. Our great politicians and our great generals have committed so many stupidities with the appearance of reasons that, perhaps,—you are reasonable under the guise of madness—but it's your life that you are sacrificing.

Pierre
I really have the right. I am alone. No one will regret me.

Bilibine
You are slandering your friends—and what about the Countess?

Pierre
Oh—my dear Bilibine! No irony! I've received a letter from the Countess in which she asks from me, in the name of my affection to fulfill for her all the formalities of divorce.

Bilibine
I swear to you I was unaware of it—in diplomacy we are ill informed.

Pierre
Why yes—she's found a very brilliant role—a young Prince of the most noble house—she already had a very high personage in the Court and doubtless would like to have married them both—

but she must choose—and she will be a Princess—oh, she had scruples— She's sought the advice of priests to know if one can remarry during the life of her husband—because she's entered the true religion.

Bilibine
The caprice of a pretty woman—

Pierre
No, indeed. The young Prince is a foreigner and a Roman Catholic. She was touched by grace and got herself instructed. She has a fine Jesuit short robe and a halo of white hairs and a pretty abbé with a long robe, all rosy and chubby like a baby. They are brave folks—they will deliver me of Countess Helene and I will be absolutely free to accomplish my act.

Voices in the Crowd
Ah! Ah! A poster! Whose!

Bilibine
Ah, why you are not alone in action! Rostopchine is showing himself too. He is writing. Let's see his patriotic eloquence—

Voices in the Crowd
Read it to us, you!

First Passerby
(Climbing on a milestone and reading) "My children. No bewilderment and no panic. Moscow will be defended until the last drop of our blood. A great affair is being prepared! The coming day I will need the young blood of the town and country"

Voices in the Crowd
We will all go.

First Passerby
(Still reading) All weapons will be good for us because it's indeed good with the axe, not bad with the pike—spear and even better with the three-toothed pitchfork

Voices in the Crowd
Hurrah! Hurrah!

First Peasant
(Still reading) Tomorrow, after dinner I shall go.

Bilibine
(To Pierre) After dinner—That'll set you up—

First Peasant
(Continuing)With the Holy Images to see the wounded and Holy Water, so they will be cured more quickly! As for me, now I indeed—well—my bad eye's much better—

Bilibine
Ah, indeed this is excellent as soon as "the Governor gives them news of his health," they believe he's truly interested in their health!

(Some officers clamber up to the landing at the top of the stairs)

Pierre
Someone's going into the Governor's It's the hour of audiences.

Bilibine
Let's go see our good father.

(They climb the stairs)

First Passerby
Oh—Listen to this "The first thing to do is to drive out the evil spirits and to send the malefactors to the devil"— We are going to put ourselves to work and end by having a good time with them.

Second Passerby
He will clear away everything—he'll settle the accounts of all the malefactors!

Second Passerby
There aren't all that many!

First Passerby
There's still Verestchaguine.

Third Peasant
We need to know if he is guilty.

Second Passerby
Now there's a question! He's a skirt chaser, a good–for-nothing without faith or law—he respects nothing—he carried off the great icon which was in his father's restaurant at The Kamenni

bridge and with a scoundrel of a painter made an abominable image of it.

Third Peasant
That's not a reason for him to have drafted the proclamation calling the French to Moscow—

First Passerby
But he admits it himself.

Third Passerby
Meaning he doesn't want to reveal those with whom he hangs out.

A Woman
But what more can be done to him? He's been condemned to forced labor.

First and Second Passerby
(together) That was well done.

A Woman
It's sad all the same! He's so young.

(The people enter—Fili returns)

Voices
Moscow is betrayed!—Moscow is lost—The Serenissimo has ordered the town abandoned. The Army is going to pass through Moscow without leaving a single man.

Shouts
We've been betrayed.

First Passerby
It's not true. Our father Koutouzov didn't order it.

Man in Crowd
Yes! The Germans didn't insist on it. But he said "It's up to My Russian noggin to decide." And he ordered the retreat.

Third Passerby
He did the right thing. He's not a traitor.

Second Passerby
Yes! But in that case why did Rostopchine say we would defend ourselves until the last drop of our blood?

First Passerby
Let him give us an accounting! Let him explain himself.

Fourth Passerby
The Lords, the merchants can leave! What about us? We will die of the situation here!

First Passerby
Are we dogs?

(Bilibine and Pierre emerge from The Governor's)

Bilibine
You see, I wasn't mistaken. Koutouzov has done his duty, and Rostopchine knows at last what he intends to do.

Pierre
And me, too.

First Passerby
(To Bilibine and Pierre) Gentlemen, you who just emerged from the Governor's—Is it true that Moscow is going to be evacuated? That—?

Bilibine
In the times we live in—everything is true!

Second Passerby
(Running) You don't know? The balloon! The balloon from Leipzig has left!

Crowd
Ah!—oh!

Second Passerby
Yes—They dismantled it! It's leaving on a 150 carts.

Crowd
Treason!

Bilibine
(To Pierre) Let's leave! This is going to get out of hand. One can perhaps carry away their army—but their plaything—

Pierre
I'm going to the Rostovs. They must have need of me! Goodbye, my dear Bilibine.

Bilibine
Au revoir, Count. In this world or the next!

(They leave)

Crowd
The Governor! The Governor! An account—Let him explain. Yes, yes, he's got to tell us. The Governor! The Governor! (The door-window on the landing opens) There he is! There he is!

Rostopchine
(Appearing—to an officer) Is my carriage ready?

Officer
It is ready, Your Excellency!

Rostopchine
Hello, my children! Hello! Thanks for coming.

Functionary
Your Excellency!

Rostopchine
I am going to be with you in a moment.

(To crowd) I will answer all your questions paternally. But, first of all I must be allowed to fulfill my responsibilities.

(To Functionary) What do you want?

First Functionary
Orders regarding my prisoners.

Rostopchine
Let them all free!

First Functionary
But, Excellency, there are political criminals! Nikonoff, Verest-chaguine.

Rostopchine
Verestchaguine? He hasn't been hanged yet? Have him brought here!

(Functionary leaves rapidly. To the crowd) And now, my children.

Second Functionary
Excellency—it's about my madmen—What's to be done with them?

Rostopchine
Let them free! Why lock them up when others run the streets!

(The Second Functionary leaves.)

Now, my children, we are going to fulfill our primary duty which is to avenge our country's malefactors! We must punish the Brigand who at the moment when you all wanted to give everything, to do everything, to save Moscow, was working to sell it out—

Voices in the Crowd
You see indeed that he is with us. But yes, it's not his fault. Punish, punish—that's the best thing to do.

Rostopchine
Here's the wretch!

Voices in the Crowd
Verestchaguine! Verestchaguine!

Rostopchine
Put him there!

(Verestchaguine is led to the first step of the landing. Profound silence. Verestchaguine keeps a resigned and sorrowful attitude, he smiles timidly at the crowd, he seeks to catch Rostopchine's glance, he seems to want to speak but the Governor avoids looking at him)

This man betrayed the Tsar and the Country. He sold himself to Bonaparte! He wanted to sell us at the same time. Alone of all the Russians he dishonored the Russian name. It's because of him Moscow perishes!

(Striking Verestchaguine suddenly with his glance) Make it your affair! I give him up to you! (Murmurs, at first hesitating in the crowd) Strike him. Let the traitor perish! Wash shame from the Russian name. Tear him to pieces! I order you.

Verestchaguine
Count! God alone is our master!

Rostopchine
Hush him, will you!

Dragoon Officer
Saber's out!

Rostopchine
Strike.

(A soldier rends a scabbard blow to Verestchaguine face)

Verestchaguine
Oh!

(Moans of horror in the crowd. Cowardly howls from the crowd respond to. Verestchaguine screams. A man seizes him by the throat and disappears with him into the crowd. Sabers and fists are raised)

Voice
Strike him with the axe. He betrayed Christ. Is this really him at least?

Rostopchine
(Withdrawing) The populace is hideous!

Voices
That's it, He got what was coming to him.

Rostopchine
My carriage. (Leaves, very upset) Ignoble, but one must do one's duty.

(He leaves)

(Enter a released madman—running)

A Woman
(Moving away) A released madman. Get the fool! Get the fool!

Fool
Wait for me! Wait for me! Ah, blood, blood Ah—popular justice is beautiful.

CURTAIN

ACT V

Scene 9

A Courtyard in front of the Rostov house. In the middle of the stage—the large oak of the third act. Its leaves are now yellow and begin to fall. To the right a gate leading to the great courtyard where the carts are hitched up. Boxes, trunks are prepared for departure. Servants come and go with different objects, packages, etc.

(Natasha and Sonia finish a trunk)

Sonia
That will never hold.

Natasha
Why, yes, why, yes! All we have to do is press a bit. Tapestries don't fear anything! Come on, push, Douniacha.

Douniacha
I'm pushing, my pigeon. I'm pushing.

Natasha
Lean, Sonia, lean! Again! There. That's it! That's it! I knew indeed that would hold.

(Count Rostov enters)

Count Rostov
Well, my darlings—it's coming along—We have to leave this very evening—don't forget it.

Natasha
You see, Papa—yet another trunk done!

Count Rostov
Why you are all red! What harm you are doing yourselves, my poor little kids.

Natasha
Ah, it's so good to have something to do. It prevents thinking.

Count Rostov
Yes, of thinking of sad things—what frightful moments.

Natasha
And then it's fun to pack! I pack very well, right, Sonia?

Sonia
You've done wonders! All the tapestries in three packing cases! There's nothing more to do but load them on the wagons.

Natasha
(To porters who enter) Go quickly, the rest of you. Take these packing cases. They are the last three. You see, Papa, we are ready.

Count Rostov
My brave children! Sonia, go tell the Countess.

(Sonia leaves)

(To Natasha) What a little general you'd make. (Noticing an officer) But here's one of your wounded looking for you! I can call them your wounded because it was your idea to open an ambulance in the house.

Natasha
You aren't pleased with it, Papa?

Count Rostov
I am enchanted, but (To the approaching officer) What do you want, Captain and what can I do to be useful to you?

Officer
Count, I have a prayer to address to you, and I beg Miss, who has already been so good to us to intercede in our favor. Don't leave me here. Allow me to leave with you, put me anywhere—in one of your carriages, with the baggage.

Orderly
Yes, Count, take pity on my officer. He cannot even march, he's completely mutilated. Let me carry him in one of the wagons.

Natasha
Oh, father, father—

Count Rostov
Why—gladly, Natasha! Have one or two wagons emptied.

Natasha
Thanks, father.

Officer
Oh! Count! What gratitude. I owe you my life.

Orderly
Oh, thanks, thanks, Excellency, my master will bless you.

Count Rostov
Fine, fine (To Natasha) Go do what's necessary. We can indeed give up some little things.

Countess Rostov
(Entering on Berg's arm) What are you talking about?

Count Rostov
What, my darling—you've had the courage to come down. How's it going?

Berg
Dear Mama's getting better.

Countess Rostov
Yes, I want to leave—but they're not leaving, it's exasperating. But why are you talking of leaving some little things?

Count Rostov
My God, yes. I want to tell you. Here—my dear little Countess—An officer came to me to ask for some wagons for the wounded. We can indeed make a small place for them. We don't need to take everything. As for them, they are our guests. It seems to me we've invited them. What do you think? We might take them—

Countess Rostov
Listen, Count, with all your prodigality, you've led us to where we are, and now you want to ruin your children's fortune. As for me, my friend, I cannot. I cannot consent. The government is here to care for the wounded. We are idiots. If you have no pity for me, at least have pity on the children.

Berg
Yes, Papa—have pity on us.

Count Berg
Well, well, since you insist on it. Call your daughter. I no longer have orders to give here. (Calling) Natasha, Natasha!

Countess Rostov
But, my friend—

Berg
Leave it to me, Mother, I will speak to her

(To Natasha, who enters) Dear Natasha, the Countess desires that the wagons not be unpacked—we cannot abandon—

Natasha
(Interrupting him) Oh, Mama! That's not possible. You cannot want such a thing. We are not like the Germans. No, Mama, little pigeon—right? You don't refuse—What can make you not take the furniture? Just look at what's taking place in the courtyard. These poor folks who thought themselves saved and who must learn that you are condemning them to death.

Countess Rostov
But—still—we cannot.

Natasha
Mama, think that if your Petia was wounded among people who....

Countess Rostov
(To Natasha) Shut up! Shut up!

(To Count) Ely—give the orders that are necessary—Let them unload the wagons as many as necessary for the wounded.

Natasha
Little mother, little pigeon, thanks.

Count Rostov
Apples don't fall far from the tree. My dear wife (He kisses her)

Natasha
Oh, Mama, Mama (Kisses her) Come father! Come father. Come order everything.

(They leave)

Berg
(Drying a tear) I am touched. This is expensive, but it's fine, it's beautiful. By the way, since you are unpacking, I'll take the opportunity to ask you again for that little Chinese table. I've spoken to you of—and which will give Vera so much pleasure. I'd like to surprise her with it. It is such a pretty Chinese table with its English lock.

Countess Rostov
Take it, my dear, take anything you want. Let's go busy ourselves with these poor folks.

(Pierre appears and stops, seeing Natasha as she gives orders to servants carrying boxes)

Natasha
Quick, quick—Put all that in the wine cellars.

(Servants leave)

Pierre
(Calling softly) Natasha

Natasha
(Going to Pierre and giving him her hands) There you are Piotr Kirilovitch. You are sweet to have come. It's so good to see a friend's face in moments like this.

Pierre
I came to see if I could be useful to you.

Natasha
You are really good, but it's all over—we are going to leave. Are you coming with us?

Pierre
No, I'm staying in Moscow.

Natasha
Ah, that's fine. That's brave. Me, too. I would have loved to stay here.

Pierre
Alas! There's nothing for women to do here. I came to say goodbye to you.

Natasha
Goodbye? But we'll see each other again.

Pierre
No, you'll never see me again.

Natasha
What do you intend to do?

Pierre
Don't ask me! I can tell those who are indifferent to me—but not those I care about.

Natasha
Oh, in that case, don't stay in Moscow! Come with us. I'd be so joyful to see you with us. I really like you, you know, Piotr Kirilovitch. You've always been so good to me, even when I acted so crazily. It's you who said the first word of pity to me "Poor little Natasha." I can still hear the sound of your voice. But why have you always been so nice to me?

Pierre
Why? Why?— Why? Because you are the daughter of my friends—because I saw you all little—because—

Natasha
What's wrong, my friend?—you are all—

Pierre
Yes, I know, I'm funny.

Natasha
No, no!—You are not funny—I find you brave and good—and when I see you there, I want to hug you.

Pierre
Natasha! Natasha! Listen—I ought not to speak—but, when I think I'll never see your dear little face again, that I'll never hear your sweet voice call me Piotr Kirilovitch, that soon the time

will come when you will have shouted "Goodbye"—it will be over, I have no more courage—I will entrust you with my secret—of my whole life—and I will say to you, "I love you."

Natasha
You love me?

Pierre
I always have—and always without daring to tell you. First of all, you were too young—and after that I saw you so high, so much above everything—so much above me, especially—and besides I loved you too much. Finally I saw that Bolkonski loved you, he too; and I encouraged his confession—and I effaced myself before the man more worthy of you! Ah, why, why didn't you understand—?

Natasha
Don't make me ashamed—

Pierre
Eh, why speak of shame! Do you know that after your break up I had a moment of joy (to himself) O my poor Bolkonski (continuing) And do you know what I said to myself when I came on his behalf to bring you your letters with your word? I said to myself "If it wasn't me, but the most witty man, the most brilliant man, the best man in the world, and if I were free, right away, at your knees, I would ask you for your love and your hand."

Natasha
My sweet Pierre.

Pierre
But I was able to impose silence on my heart and even now, if some hope had remained, I would have said nothing. But everything is over on his side, everything is over on mine—I haven't the courage to disappear without your knowing that there was a poor lad who lived through you and for you.

Natasha
Pierre! Pierre! Come! Leave with us. Don't abandon me. Perhaps we can be happy together.

Pierre
No, no—for me happiness can only be a dream—the last.

(A soldier on a stretcher enters)

Soldier
Miss! They told us you were giving asylum to the wounded. Would you be willing to receive our Officer?

Natasha
Why certainly! Come in! Come in!

Soldier
Oh thanks, Miss—In his condition we would never have been able to take him to the square.

Natasha
Is he as bad as all that? (She goes to the curtain and pulls it back, lets out a scream and seeks refuge in Pierre's arms) Bolkonski!

Prince André
(Rising) You! What happiness (he stretches his hand to her).

Natasha
Pardon.

Prince André
I love you!

Natasha
Forgive me.

Prince André
Forgive you for what?

Natasha
(Leaning over his hand) Forgive me for what—I did!

Prince André
(Raising her face and looking at her with expression of compassion and joy) I love you better than before. My love is not of the sort that can take offence. It's not earthly love, the love of human desire—It's divine love. The love of God in all that he has done, and he's done nothing which is more dear to me than my Natasha and my Pierre! Oh—the joy of leaving life between you two!

Natasha
Don't talk like that!

Pierre
My friend, you will live.

Prince André
No, I'm condemned! My strength is worn out. Listen—opening my eyes I saw Natasha in Pierre's arms. That's your place, Natasha you must stay there.

Natasha
Oh—André—

Pierre
No, no, she's not for me.

Prince André
Your voice betrays you, Pierre, and I've finally understood everything. Yes, yes—I remember how you spoke to me of her—I understand your tenderness, your sacrifice. My friend, now I'm the one who gives her to you—who entrusts her to you. Watch over her. Fulfill your duty. Do yours for love of me.

Pierre
No, André, no. I haven't the right. I no longer belong to myself. I have a mission to fulfill, a mission of death in which I am sure to die.

(Low to André) The day of his entry to Moscow, I will strike the tyrant of mankind and I will deliver my country—

Prince André
Not that, not that, Pierre! What need have you to strike? Don't you see that the enemy is already an enraged beast who has received a mortal wound! Leave him to his fate. Pierre, don't soil our honor. Don't soil our victory! And you, Natasha, forbid him to die. Oh come! Come! Let me see you, as I saw you just now—in each others arms. (He joins their hands) Oh—be blessed for the peace and light you are giving me. Both of you be blessed. But how they are falling, the leaves from an old tree—from the tree of my life. (Trying to count them) One—another—yet another Pierre—Natasha

(He dies)

Pierre and Natasha
André!

CURTAIN

ACT V

Scene 10

A large open tent. In the back a view of Moscow.

Napoleon
(In the midst of the tent and his officers, looking at Moscow) Holy Moscow. There it is at last, this famous city. The Asian city with numberless churches. There it is at last. Just in time! See how it shines in the sun. How its thousand colors dazzle. It's like a beautiful oriental woman in lying at my feet—and awaiting her fate. And it is ours, the city of the Tsars. A gesture of my hand and it would be annihilated. Despite all the resplendent gold of its cupolas—its glory is tarnished —for a city in which the conqueror has entered is like a woman who has lost her honor—My conquest—My slave—Well, this is my response to skeptics, to those who spoke of retreating, and the reward of my soldiers. We marched and here we are at the end. Gentlemen, go find the Boyars

(Several officers leave) I will await their deputation here.

An Officer
(Entering) Sire, the Prefect of the Imperial Palace.

Napoleon
Ah, Count Beausset!

Beausset
(Followed by a servant with a covered painting which he places on a chair) Sire, I wanted to rejoin you sooner, but your eagle flies so fast.

Napoleon
I regret, Count, leaving made you come so far, but you arrive at a fine moment.

Beausset
Sire, I didn't expect, at least, to find you at the gates of Moscow.

Napoleon
You are going to see such a beautiful city. But quickly, the news—the Empress!

Beausset
Sire, I bring to Your Majesty with the compliments of Her Majesty the Empress—the regret of Paris. Paris can only console itself for its Emperor's absence by celebrating His victories. What illuminations. What fires of joy there will be when it learns—

Napoleon
(Pointing to the veiled painting) But, tell me, Count, what have you brought us, there?

Beausset
Sire, a gift from the Empress to Your Majesty.

Napoleon
Dear Empress! (Uncovering the picture) The King of Rome.

Beausset
It's a painting by Gerard.

Napoleon
Admirable! My son! What a motherly and wifely heart has the Empress! To send me the picture of my son to the army! To associate to our glory the heir of our family. We'll expose it in front of my tent. I want my Old Guard to have its share in my happiness! How happy I am! (Looking at the picture) It dictates my conduct. The Muscovites will find a father in me. My clemency is always prompt to descend on the vanquished!

(To Beausset) I'm waiting for the Boyars! They are going to bring me the keys to the city.

(To Generals) We know this ceremony! We've entered Milan, Vienna, Berlin, Madrid. Come on, my friends, yet another capital—we are going to enter her as in to other conquered cities. We are going to pass through paved streets! Flowers are going to fall on your uniforms—and women will smile on my old grumblers. Oh—look at all these birds flying joyously while the cupolas sparkle! Beausset! As soon as I return I will give orders to restore the Dome of the Invalids with gold. Come on—we'll show these good folks French magnanimity—on the old monuments of barbarism and despotism.—We will write the great words—Justice and Mercy—from the heights of the Kremlin—yes, it's at the Kremlin down there that I shall give them equitable laws. I will teach them true civilization. They have charitable institutions—We will endow them and we will call them "House of my Mother" I will force generations of Boyars to pronounce the name of their conqueror with love. And Alexander himself. But where is he at this time? And what's he doing? Alexander as he submits to the conditions that victory gives me the right to dictate to him—I will recognize that I've made war—not on him whom I admire and respect, but on the odious politics of his court. And peace, in Moscow, will flourish under our hands! World peace! We will form a Holy alliance between sovereigns! No more war! All nations will be united under our wise domination. And the European system will be founded. (Looking at the portrait) It's you, my son, who will be at the summit of all that. Paris, capital of the world, will be your capital.

(Sits and contemplates the portrait of his son. Generals enter sad and embarrassed)

First General
I will never dare.

Second General
No, it cannot be—

Third General
He has to be told all the same.

Napoleon
(Turning) Ah—the deputation!—Show the Boyars in. I shall be pleased to speak to them—

Firs General
Sire—

Napoleon
Well—what? What's wrong?

Second General
Sire—There is no deputation—Moscow is empty.

Napoleon
What are you saying?

Second General
Yes, empty.

Napoleon
Come on, will you. That's crazy! That's impossible! You are mad!

First General
Sire! It's the truth. There remain neither leaders nor magistrates—in the streets, some pillagers.

Napoleon
Moscow empty, empty—(Getting control of himself) Well, gentlemen we will ourselves be witnesses of our glory

A General
What's that light down there? Fire!

Another General
Yes—fire—and yet another one. Oh—how the flame spreads. See those birds driven out by the flames are turning on us.

Napoleon
Vultures!

CURTAIN

ABOUT FRANK J. MORLOCK

FRANK J. MORLOCK has written and translated many plays since retiring from the legal profession in 1992. His translations have also appeared on Project Gutenberg, the Alexandre Dumas Père web page, Literature in the Age of Napoléon, Infinite Artistries.com, and Munsey's (formerly Blackmask). In 2006 he received an award from the North American Jules Verne Society for his translations of Verne's plays. He lives and works in México.

www.ingramcontent.com/pod-product-compliance
Lightning Source LLC
LaVergne TN
LVHW041624070426
835507LV00008B/443